THE
WORKING
MUSICIAN

ESSENTIALS OF THE MUSIC
BUSINESS FOR NEW ARTISTS

by

GENEVIEVE BURGESS

ISBN: 0615689531
ISBN-13: 9780615689531

Library of Congress Control Number: 2012948022
Burgess Publishing, Westminster, MD

TABLE OF CONTENTS

INTRODUCTION

*I*ndependent (or sometimes *indie*) is a word that has been bandied about in
the entertainment world in the last decade. It means different things
to different people—freedom from contracts and oppressive label poli-
cies, music you won't hear on the radio, low-budget movies, musicians
who have created their own companies that work in conjunction with or
separate from a major label, small record labels, and more. Many have said
that the future of the music industry lies with independent artists, rather
than with record labels, and have encouraged artists to take their careers
into their own hands, even artists who are currently with labels. It sounds
great. Cut out the middleman! Interact directly with fans! Be your own
boss! What's the catch?

The catch is that most artists who may be good at writing and performing music probably aren't also good at marketing, PR, booking, distribution, accounting, coordinating tours, merchandizing, and utilizing social
media. The catch is that playing at your local bar, selling your CD out of
the trunk of your car, and selling some downloads here and there through
CD Baby or TuneCore makes it nearly impossible to earn the money necessary to go on tour or professionally record a CD. The catch is that pinning
your hopes on going viral is like singing in your shower and hoping Simon

Cowell walks by your open window and discovers you. The catch is that putting the onus on the artists to sell themselves is a good way to ignore the larger problems in the way the music industry has done business and how they expect to keep doing business. Putting up a MySpace page and collecting Facebook fans is a great start, but unless you have a real business plan behind it, it won't get you anywhere.

The theory of the independent artist is an attractive one, but how feasible is it? Can one person claw his or her way up from playing on street corners to selling out stadiums without a label, manager, or booking agent? For those who are independent, how is it working for them? What's the actual business model for an independent artist? What are the experiences of those who are independent, and how does the experience of bands that have left their labels and gone into business for themselves compare to those that have never been signed and have learned to manage themselves for lack of a better option? If the future of the music industry is the independent artist, then someone needs to figure out what that actually means. By and large, artists have never been expected to be good businesspeople, which is why the ones who are (Jimmy Buffett, Dolly Parton, Gene Simmons, Prince, et al.) are seen as exceptional rather than the rule. If the expectation now is that artists should manage their own careers, then they need the information on how to do that.

Furthermore, artists need to be aware of all aspects of the industry. Whereas once the record company would take care of the business side for you, artists who embark on an independent career now need to be aware of copyright law, basic music-publishing deals, how to read a contract, and what resources are out there to help them succeed. Because it is so easy to put up MySpace and Facebook pages, get yourself signed up for TuneCore or CD Baby, and build a website, there are a lot of bands out there that have those things working for them already, so what sets a band apart in the minds of fans? Or in the minds of corporate sponsors?

INTRODUCTION

The goal of this book is to condense a wide amount of information and speculation about the music industry and to tackle in a broad sense many of the topics that independent artists will face. I can't tell any musician how to launch his or her career, but I can tell you what resources are out there, how others have utilized them, and some common mistakes or misunderstandings to avoid. Going into business for yourself is a big decision no matter what industry you're in, and choosing to promote yourself as an artist is going into business whether or not you like to think of it that way.

Additionally, being a fan of an independent artist requires fans to adjust their expectations of the kind of support musicians need. Whereas once it was enough to buy albums, go to their concerts, and maybe buy a T-shirt or two, fans of independent artists are finding that now they're asked to be far more involved in their support. Being asked for donations to fund the making of an album, calling to request their songs on local radio stations, even helping artists find venues, for example, fans can be a bigger help to their favorite artists than ever before. Some fans may balk at being asked to participate in an artist's creative ventures on ArtistShare or Kickstarter, but a deeper understanding of how the business has changed for artists may help these fans see why their support is more vital and more deeply appreciated than it would be for label artists.

That doesn't mean there's not fun to be had in the music world. We've reached a point where buying a computer can give anyone the tools to put their music or movies on the Internet quickly and easily. You can find music and purchase it within minutes. You can listen to radio stations from around the world through streams on websites. It's an amazing time to be a musician or a music fan if only because of the creative opportunities that are so readily available. The trick is to make the best of those opportunities when they come along.

CHAPTER 1:

GAMING THE SYSTEM

Throughout the history of the music industry (or as long as music has existed as a commodity) there have been musicians, composers, and performers who have risen to the task of managing their own business affairs rather than relying on the help of others. A few of them managed not to fail spectacularly.

Indeed, for most of history, those who are performers or artists of some kind have been assumed to be incompetent in matters of business, the idea being that the very quality that makes them so creative also makes them unable to deal with such concrete matters as contracts or money. Artists lived in a world beyond those things, it was thought, a place where the muses spoke to them and financial compensation was not even an afterthought. It wasn't until the modern era that music even became a business on its own rather than something funded by the church, nobles, royalty, or other wealthy patrons for their own amusement. Once the modern music business was born in Tin Pan Alley, though, some musicians managed to distinguish themselves not only as talented artists but also as shrewd businesspeople. Even into the modern music era, most artists were told to stay out of the business side of music, and the vast majority of them were content with that arrangement until they went bankrupt. In the past few decades, there have been some noteworthy artists who have stood out in how they have handled their business affairs as well as their creative output.

Once upon a time, no one even knew what Gene Simmons looked like, despite the fact that he fronted one of the largest bands of the '70s. His signature demon make-up didn't come off until 1983, when the band's popularity began to wane. Currently, there are many younger people who are more likely to know Simmons for his reality series, *Gene Simmons Family Jewels*, in which he stars with longtime companion (now wife) Shannon Tweed and their two children, Nick and Sophie. Mr. Simmons is currently going on four decades as a celebrity, and he shows no signs of stopping. Part of this is because of his willingness to merchandise anything (KISS condoms, anyone?), but part of it is also because he has dedication and business acumen beyond that of the average rock star.

KISS fought their way to fame. A feature in the October 3, 2009, issue of *Billboard* describes the band's early days and the struggle they had to achieve legitimacy in the eyes of the music industry. While it sounds incredible now, the hard-rocking band was initially shunned by the tastemakers of the music industry. Their music wasn't played on the radio, and critics slammed their work, so their first fans learned about them entirely through word of mouth. They went viral decades before the Internet existed. Their shows were their calling card, and, when they launched their first national tour in 1974, they were selling out stadiums before they had their first hit song on the radio. In 1975 the live version of "Rock and Roll All Nite" went to number twelve on the *Billboard* Hot 100, and the legacy of KISS as rock-and-roll royalty had begun. As their fame increased, their shows became more theatrical, with pyrotechnics, hydraulics, and fake blood being prominent features. Their 1976 album, *Destroyer*, went platinum, and by 1980 the band's success was legendary—as was the slavish devotion of their fans, both the ones who had been there since the beginning and those who were impressed along the way by the band's indescribable live shows. The KISS Army, as they became known, was a big reason behind the band's success with tours and with their later merchandising efforts.

In an interview with *Business Week* magazine in September 2008, Simmons discussed how he first began to look outside of music for business, saying, "When the band was first starting off, we noticed that T-shirts and non-music items were earning a substantial amount of money. KISS quickly became a multi-headed beast: rock band and rock 'n' roll brand—and the only one to have endured the ages and decades of fads and fashions. Today we have three thousand licensed products, everything from condoms to caskets."[1] When asked, "How do you identify a business opportunity?" Simmons replied, "I trust my gut. I have to have an emotional connection to what I am ultimately selling because it is emotion, whether you are selling religion, politics, even a breath mint." These tips hold very true for artists today, many of whom will see far more money coming in from non-music-related merchandise than they will from album sales. And while I am skeptical that Mr. Simmons has a deep, personal connection to every one of those three thousand products that are carrying the KISS brand on them, his advice to look for a connection is a good one. Because independent artists are more connected with their fans, the chance to collect information about what products they'd like you to offer is never more than a Facebook or Twitter post away, and services like Cafepress and Zazzle, which offer print-on-demand merchandise, are a great way to sell merchandise without huge up-front costs.

There are two things that Dolly Parton is best known for, and neither of them is her business sense. However, to overlook the other endowments that the petite Tennessee native brings to the table would be foolish. Since the late '60s, Dolly Parton has been a part of the country music landscape and has expanded her career to the point that she is now the head of an

---

1 The aforementioned *Billboard* feature lists this number as five thousand licensed products.

empire that includes a theme park, a film and television production company, her own record company, and several other business ventures. She's been a Kennedy Center honoree, was awarded a Living Legend Medal by the US Library of Congress, received a National Medal of Arts from the US government, has been nominated for Academy Awards, Tonys, and has won eight Grammys out of a total of forty-five nominations. In 2001 she earned the *Good Housekeeping* Seal of Approval, marking the first time that title had been awarded to a person. A full list of the other honors she has been awarded or nominated for could take up the rest of this chapter. In short, her cup size may be the least impressive thing about Dolly Parton.

Part of what has made Ms. Parton an enduring success is that she's not just a singer, she's an extremely talented songwriter, and she's held on to the copyrights to her songs even when it seemed foolish to do so. The most famous example is her ballad "I Will Always Love You." After she had recorded the song and earned a hit with it in 1974 (her version made it to number one on the *Billboard* Hot Country Songs chart that year), Elvis Presley announced his intention to record the song. Parton was thrilled—until his manager, Colonel Tom Parker, told Parton that a condition of Elvis's recording her song would be that she had to sign 50 percent ownership of the copyright over to Elvis and Parker. Parton later related that she told Parker that she wouldn't do it because the publishing royalties she received from the song were for her family even after her death, so she couldn't give up half of the publishing income. Elvis never recorded the song and Parton maintained full ownership of the song, though at the time many around her thought she was a fool to turn down the opportunity.[2] Parton got the last laugh, though, as Whitney Houston's cover of "I Will Always Love You" released in conjunction with the movie *The Bodyguard* became the biggest selling single by a female artist until that point in time, and Parton earned her full royalty on every single copy sold. Beyond that, as a songwriter she earned royalties every time the song was played on the

2 "Dolly wasn't parton with hit song", Joan McGurk, *Belfast Telegraph*, March 26th, 2007.

radio and anytime the film was shown in television or theaters. Houston's version also helped make the song an enduring standard, meaning there are likely many more covers to come and more royalties for Ms. Parton in the future. Copyrights are some of the most valuable things that songwriters and artists will ever have, and Ms. Parton's example should show how important it is to hang onto your interest in these assets. While you're going to share royalties if you co-wrote a single with someone, you should never sign even part of your copyright over to someone else who isn't involved in the creative process. It gives them access to royalties that are meant to be due specifically to songwriters as well as a say in how the song gets used in the future—whether or not the songwriter is singing it. In the case of "I Will Always Love You," this means that it's possible that if Ms. Parton had signed over 50 percent of the copyright, the Presley estate could have blocked the use of the song in *The Bodyguard*, and the song would have had a very different history.

Dolly Parton's career has maintained momentum through four decades and she shows no signs of stopping. Part of her lasting success can be chalked up to her ability to cultivate business opportunities outside of music, but her public persona remains that of an entertainer first and foremost. Music gave Ms. Parton the foot in the door and name recognition that gave her the ability to branch out into all her other various business ventures. By making good decisions about her career and the assets she had available to her, she's crafted an empire. Dolly Parton is a formidable businesswoman who doesn't show any signs of slowing down.

Few of us who lived through the '90s can forget the epic battle that Prince (later to be known as "The Artist Formerly Known as Prince" and then still later as Prince once again) waged against Warner Brothers over a contract dispute. After he left Warner Brothers in 1996, Prince began a career the likes of which had not yet been seen: using the Internet to self-distribute, arranging distribution deals with record labels for single albums rather than signing lengthy contracts, and even giving albums away with the purchase of a concert ticket. Before the world realized that selling a CD with ten to twelve songs on it at the local record store wasn't going to be a big moneymaker anymore, Prince had already built a business plan that cast a broader net for revenue sources.

After leaving Warner Brothers, Prince recorded music in his home studio and released it directly to fans through his website during the infancy of the Internet. While there were problems with the distribution model, Prince kept the vast majority of the money the fans paid for the album rather than the standard 10 percent he would have gotten under a major label contract. For his album *Musicology* he did end up licensing the album for major label distribution, but he also gave copies of it away for free to anyone who bought a ticket to his arena tour that year. The album "sold" far more copies as part of the ticket package than it did as a stand-alone album. Later, he licensed the album *Planet Earth* to be given away to subscribers of London's *Daily Mail* as a promotion for his twenty-one show residency at the O2 arena. While Prince lost money on the album, he made all of that and much more back on ticket sales. Free of his record label contract, Prince was able to devote his time and energy where he wanted—frequently creating new music and touring extensively.[3] Even that's changed recently, though. In an interview with *The Guardian* in June 2011, Prince stated that he would not release any more recordings for the time being due to the threat of piracy. As he put it, "We made money before piracy was real crazy. Nobody's making money now except phone companies, Apple, and Google. I'm supposed to go to the White House to talk about copyright protection. It's like the gold rush out there. Or a carjacking. There's no boundaries. I've been in meetings, and they tell you, Prince you don't understand, it's dog-eat-dog out there. So I'll just hold off on recording." Despite being down on the Internet, Prince proved that artists can find success without a major label backing them. And even though he's backed

---

3 *Ripped: How the Wired Generation Revolutionized Music* by Greg Kot. Scribner, New York, 2009. Pg. 58-64.

away from recording for now, his early adoption of the Internet as a direct distribution model was groundbreaking and helped further the cause of the independent artist.

One of the artists who immediately springs to mind when you talk about business is Jimmy Buffett. Mr. Buffett managed to turn his laid-back songs extolling the virtues of a nice sunset, a frosty drink, and a good feeling about the world into a corporate empire that includes restaurants, liquor, beer, clothing, and an entire lifestyle with devotees no less fervent than those of the Grateful Dead. He's built a reputation and an empire on a solid fan base.

Jimmy Buffett's music career began in 1969 when he moved to New Orleans and began playing clubs on Bourbon Street with a cover band called Upstairs Alliance. After a few missteps, he moved to Key West and ended up with a recording contract with ABC Records. He recorded *A White Sport Coat and a Pink Crustacean* in Nashville and followed up with *Living and Dying in 3/4 Time*. The second album had the single "Come Monday" and Buffett's career was up and rolling. As of 2011, Buffet has produced twenty-six studio albums, eleven live albums, and sixty-seven singles. Five of his albums are certified platinum, and five are certified gold. Prior to 1994 only one of Buffet's studio albums, *Changes in Latitudes, Changes in Attitudes*, managed to crack the top ten on the US charts and that one came in right at number ten. In contrast, in the '90s Buffet released five albums and four of them broke the top ten. His only number one selling album was released in 2004. As for his singles, the highest any of them reached on the *Billboard* Hot 100 was number eight, and that was for the song "Margaritaville." Clearly, Buffett's prolific career could be best categorized as a slow burn rather than a hot commodity, which makes it all the more impressive that he managed to not only achieve such a high level of success but also managed to maintain that level of success for over forty years.

While his albums are frequently listed in the country category, it's not quite a perfect fit. While the laid-back sound of twangy guitars and the songs built around stories are well at home in country's wheelhouse, there's something a little extra to Buffett's songs that place him in a league of his own. Until *Billboard* creates a "Caribbean-influenced country" category, though, it's probably the best fit Buffett's work is likely to find. Perhaps his unique sound is what made him stand out to fans around the world and has earned him continued success in his touring career. Part of the reason Buffett's tours have been so successful can be traced back to the fact that Buffett has a list of popular tunes that he plays at virtually every live performance. While many artists can come to resent their big hits in some way and refuse to perform them live, Buffett seems to embrace the fame of songs like "Margaritaville" and "Cheeseburger in Paradise" and is not shy about giving the people what they want. His dedicated legions of fans call themselves Parrot Heads and gather in parking lots, not unlike the fans of the Grateful Dead (but with more hula skirts and Hawaiian shirts). Buffett's songs aren't just catchy tunes that you can dance to; he's turned them into a culture and, more important from a business perspective, a brand.

The Margaritaville brand has expanded to include hotels, cafés, restaurants, a clothing line, a food line, a radio station on SiriusXM, a line of patio furniture, eyewear, a Facebook game (Margaritaville online) by interactive game giant THQ, and a custom margarita blender. Buffett also owns the Landshark lager brand. It's clear that his particular kind of business expertise extends beyond the music world. While his success grew out of the super-fan Parrot Heads, though, many of the people who purchase the items that populate the Jimmy Buffett empire may not be aware of their origin. Building a brand is about more than appealing to your most rabid fans; it's about finding ways to create products where you can remove your influence from the equation and still have a successful product. The percentage of Americans who drink lager is much larger than the percentage of Americans who are Parrot Heads, so while marketing to the latter was a good way to get up and rolling, it's marketing to the former that's going to keep the business alive.

It's clear that Buffett's success is due in strong part to a central brand that he's able to market to super- and casual fans, but that doesn't mean that groups who are just starting out should focus their efforts on creating a brand. Buffett's career had grown for years before he became more Jimmy Buffett the brand than Jimmy Buffett the artist. His music and touring efforts allowed him the freedom to expand into other business ventures and create a brand for himself, not vice versa. At a SXSW panel on branding in March 2012, the overall message was that branding should happen organically. As Kevin Liles, the former president of Def Jam, said, "Brands don't happen overnight.... What bothers me about brand-building is that everyone wants to be a brand." What young artists should take away from the example of Jimmy Buffett is not to create a brand to build their music around, but that if the music is good, the fans will come, and a brand or image will emerge. Don't write songs trying to figure out what the product tie-in will be—write the song and the tie-ins will become apparent.

Most of those artists got their start with a label and later began working the business side on their own after they had achieved success. Is there an example of a band that has worked their way up independently? There is indeed. Meet The String Cheese Incident, a band that started their own record label in 1998 in order to record their music and their own ticket company to sell tickets to their shows directly to fans. In fact, it was probably their ability to start these businesses and run them successfully that helped build their career by making their albums and tickets available to fans directly through their website. This ensured that web traffic stayed with them and their site collected the relevant data on fans who were purchasing their albums and tickets. Recently they announced that for their 2012 summer tour, "the ticket price that is listed is the price that you will pay," combatting the ticketing trend of adding extra charges and fees during checkout to ticket prices if the tickets are ordered through their website. This is because the band has agreed to cover the credit card and the cost of handling in order to give fans a hassle-free ticket purchase. Moves like this can make performers a lot of friends within their fan base, who will see the artist as more ideologically aligned with their own values (in this case, paying an advertised price without add-ons) and deepen the connection the fan feels with the artist. Comedian Louis C.K. did something similar for his 2012 fall tour, selling tickets for forty-five dollars apiece on his website directly to fans. He ended up selling 135,600 tickets in one week, earning over $6 million in gross sales[4]. Listen to your fans, and always keep feelers out there for what people are thinking about your business model. While most ideas might not be feasible, finding ways to implement the ones that are can have long-term benefits in the way your fans perceive you.

Other artists are also beginning to explore the advantages of independence. Former Fleetwood Mac front man Lindsey Buckingham is releasing his latest solo album independently. This will be the first independent album for Buckingham, whose career has spanned four decades. The band Garbage has also decided to release their upcoming album independently, after recording it independently and making the decision not to sell it to a major label upon completion. Bonnie Raitt is another notable artist who has announced her intentions to release music independently. In some of these cases, "independently" means that the artists have started their own label, and in other cases that they're working with small, independent record labels. There are limitations to this approach; for their upcoming tour, Garbage has no up-front support and will be able to keep touring only as long as they're selling tickets[5]. But there are many artists who relish the creative control that independence offers. In fact, in the next several years, it is possible that a greater number of established artists will take more of the business side of their careers into their own hands. In the Copyright Act of 1976, there was a provision that allowed copyright holders or their heirs to reclaim full rights to their copyrighted material, no matter what

---

4 Techdirt.com, "Louis CK's Direct Tour Sales: Over $6 Million in 1 Week, Scalping Drops from 25% to Below 1%" Mike Masnick July 5th, 2012.
5 *Billboard,* August 2011.

the original contract said, after a certain period of time. For songs that were copyrighted in 1978 or after, the reclamation window opens thirty-five years after the copyright was registered, so the works can be "recaptured" in 2013. The window for notification of intent to reclaim copyrights, though, has already opened, and there are artists or artists' heirs who are making their intentions to reclaim their copyrights known. At the very least, the possibility that artists can take back their copyright can give artists the chance to negotiate more favorable terms or move their copyrights to a company willing to offer them better terms.

In addition to artists who have taken creative control of their own careers, there are also countless artists who have used their fame and clout in the industry to start their own record labels. Usually the labels exist as an offshoot of a larger label and are known as vanity labels, but anything that gets an artist on the business side of a record is going to be more profitable than being just an artist. Some vanity labels have grown to be real moneymakers for the artists who started them and the record companies that they're attached to, such as Young Money Entertainment, which was started by Lil Wayne and has signed Nicki Minaj and Drake. Young Money is operated by Cash Money Records, which is itself part of the Universal Music Group. Some artists who start labels do so because they're interested in finding new talent and giving those artists a place to shine. Some artists start their own labels because they want to have more say in their record development and more freedom to control the process of making and releasing an album. Sometimes it's a pure business decision: if the artist is getting artist royalties and a cut of the record label royalties by releasing an album on their "own" label, their bottom line looks a lot nicer at the end of the day.

Right now it's far easier to launch an album than it ever was, but much harder to gain access to the kind of resources that some of these artists had behind them when they began their careers. While they were able to capitalize on their success in ways that artists with less business acumen couldn't, they were also able to take advantage of many services that labels, which gave them time to build their careers over the course of years and albums, were happy to provide to them. The way labels did business has a lot to do with how record labels got started in the first place, and that's a story that will take us back before records even existed. What follows is sort of a whirlwind tour of the history of the music industry in America, which I hope will give you some insights into how things ended up the way they did and where they might be going in the future.

CHAPTER 2:

THE EVOLUTION OF DISTRIBUTION

O nce upon a time, the greatest hurdle a band had to overcome in their career was the problem of distribution. Almost anyone can pick up an instrument and learn to play, and a select few people can learn to play very well and perform in front of others. But how do you get those performances to people who aren't in your immediate vicinity? Obviously, time was that you just didn't, and there was a very different culture that revolved around the trade of sheet music, with every town having at least a handful of talented musicians who could bang out a rousing tune on the piano or fiddle when called upon. Now we have music that can be accessed on demand anywhere you can find Internet or cell phone service, and technology that makes it possible to carry weeks' worth of songs on a device small enough to fit in one's pocket. So how did we get from point A to point B, and how many times did the music business seem on the verge of collapse in between?

Learning the history of music distribution can also help clarify some of the stranger customs and terms still used in the music-publishing world. We still use the term *mechanicals* for mechanical royalties or royalties due on copies of music that are to be played by a device, because the provision in the copyright law that allowed those royalties to be collected was written when player pianos were in vogue, and it specifically related to the sales of copies of music that were to be played via mechanical means rather than sheet music meant to be played and/or sung by live performers. Then, mechanical music production was the exception; now it's the rule, and some of the language in the copyright law is a little outdated.

The first version of commercial music production in the US was the printing and publishing of sheet music. A lot of the terms from this era are still around today, most notably the fact that the side of the industry that deals with copyright ownership and licensing is routinely referred to as publishing, despite the fact that it has little connection to the traditional sense of the word anymore. Popular music as we know it can be traced back to the music publishers and songwriters who established themselves in New York City in the late nineteenth century in an area that would become known as Tin Pan Alley. This industry began pumping out short, catchy tunes meant to be played on piano and sung by a solo singer with a chorus that was easy to identify and remember, so friends could join in the singing, most of which was not exceptionally difficult, so the music could be shipped out to piano players all over the country. It was a new genre, something different than orchestra music, musicals, operas, or hymns and spirituals such as one might hear at church. The subjects and compositions were hardly groundbreaking, but they represented a new version of music that was meant to be played and performed largely by amateurs for fun rather than for any kind of specific cultural value.

"To maximize profits, publishers sought to minimize financial risk and sell to as large a market as possible. Songs based on a previously successful formula appealed to them, because they knew a market for this kind of product already existed. And for consumers, formulas held appeal as well; in a stressful world with a dizzying array of consumer choices, purchasers could know what they were getting and could expect not to be disappointed."[6]

6 David Suisman, *Selling Sounds*, Harvard University Press, 2009, pg. 48.

The above quote may sound like something that would be said about the current music climate; it was actually describing the business tactics pioneered by the Tin Pan Alley song publishers in the beginning of the twentieth century. The way songs were sold in this era is something that sounds amazing to consumers today; song pluggers (usually otherwise unemployed pianists and singers) would receive free copies of the songs from the publishers and would stage free performances in public areas, usually with "chorus sheets" printed on cheap paper that could be handed out to observers to induce them to sing along with the chorus. These sheets also conveniently contained the name of the song and the name of the publisher, so the audience could easily find the song to purchase it later. Sheet music had its own counter in large department stores, which usually had a stage set up for the song pluggers to perform on, and these same song pluggers tended to use a special method to get the counter girls to push their publisher's songs in a tradition that's existed nearly as long as people have paid to listen to music: bribery. Song pluggers would also stage free performances at cinemas, lounges, parks—nearly anywhere people gathered. All music was performed live for the benefit of consumers, with frequent entreaties to get them to join in singing.

Of course, once this fledgling music industry was established, it was immediately besieged by accusations of fraud, greed, underhanded dealings, intellectual property theft, and mistreatment of artists. Shockingly, many of these allegations proved to be true. Not only that, but it also wasn't long before a new format came along to disrupt all the carefully organized cons that the executives in the publishing industry had established for themselves, sending them running to various legislators to block this new technology from damaging their industry. In this case it was the development of the phonograph. No longer did consumers have to purchase sheet music in order to listen to popular songs; now they could put on a record and save themselves or their friends the trouble of learning the words and music. More importantly, the phonograph could capture an artist or performing group once and make that performance available to millions, regardless of geography.

The record industry started with the invention of the phonograph by Thomas Edison in 1877. The original phonograph worked with a wax cylinder rather than the familiar flat disc. Emile Berliner developed that disc around the turn of the century, and the gramophone we recognize today was born. Player pianos were also developed in 1876 and were more popular in the early twentieth century, as they were considered more innovative. Record companies had to find a way to distinguish themselves and get Americans away from the piano, and the Victor Talking Machine Company found a way to do that when they partnered with the Gramophone Company in England to launch a series of records referred to as the Red Seal records. These records were recordings of internationally renowned musicians, composers, or orchestras that were sold at a much higher price that the regular or "Black Seal" records by the same companies. One of the most famous partnerships to come out of the Red Seal records was that of the Victor Company and Enrico Caruso, the famous Italian tenor.

Without the Red Seal line, which became something of a status symbol and elevated records to the level of high culture in the eyes of many consumers, the record industry may well have faltered out of the gate. Phonograph cylinders allowed consumers to not only listen to prerecorded works but also to record their own cylinders. But the phonograph and records overall were seen as culturally inferior to player pianos and the more advanced reproducing pianos, which not only played music from mechanical scrolls but could replicate dynamics and tempo changes to give listeners the nearest approximation to a live, professional performance at the time. The advantages over recorded piano music are easy to see, as even mechanically performed piano music will sound better on a live piano than the version that ends up on a record. Ultimately records became the dominant form of recorded music, and certain limitations of the medium ended up influencing the music that became popular not only in the early years of the twentieth century but also for decades afterward; since recording strings was difficult, record companies would push recordings made by brass bands or pianos. Vocal music also became popular, though only in certain ranges that seemed to work well with the recording process. Caruso and other tenors began to supplant the traditional opera stars, female sopranos, because it was incredibly difficult to record a soprano's voice clearly. Time limitations on records meant that longer works were abridged, or shorter pieces were selected for recording and elevated to the level of "classics" by the marketing departments of record companies. The sale of records exploded, and their reign continued through the greater part of the twentieth century.

The marketing of the Red Seal records also helped introduce a technique that would be common for the rest of the twentieth century and perhaps a hallmark of the music industry for the rest of time: selling an image, a concept that had a loose connection to the actual product. Red Seal recordings were positioned as symbols of class, culture, and refinement. They were aspirational objects for many who bought them, a representation of the idealized images of themselves that people had. Record companies have never stopped selling images, though the images have shifted from one of culture and class to whatever the times required.

Looking at the history of the music business, it's clear that the hysteria surrounding digital distribution in the early years of the twenty-first century was something which was entirely predictable, based on the industry's previous reactions to almost everything that has ever happened to the music industry in America. Any advance in technology was immediately seen as a threat rather than an opportunity, and battles have been fought every step of the way, even with technologies that later proved remarkably beneficial to the music industry. One of the first big fights was between record makers and radio, because record labels felt that radio would impede sales of records. In 1929 a band leader sued his record label when he learned his records were being played on the radio, on the basis that recordings of his music being played on the radio damaged his earning potential and put him in the position of competing with himself. *Paul Whiteman v. RCA Manufacturing Company* was originally decided in favor of Whiteman, with the district court ruling that "the very nature of the phonograph record indicates the limited form of its publication. It was intended for listeners of a phonograph, not for a radio audience.... Broadcast stations can give their public Whiteman's orchestra, by hiring the orchestra at a proper prices as some of them do." The case was appealed by RCA to grant them remedies from the radio stationed named in the suit as well. The case was first heard in 1939 and the appeal in 1940.[7] Given the payola that categorized the mid to late years of the twentieth century, it's interesting to see examples of artists and record companies actively fighting for radio stations to *not* play their music, but not surprising. Of course, they swiftly figured out that radio could be used as a very lucrative promotion method, and a much friendlier relationship was forged. Until it made them money, it wasn't in their best interest, and once it did make them money, it became a race to see who could exploit the medium most thoroughly.

Fast-forward a few decades to the year CDs entered the US market, 1983, when a grand total of eight hundred thousand of them were sold in the US. By 1990 there were a total of 288 million sold. As CDs became more popular and the hardware to play them became nearly ubiquitous, the record companies began to phase out alternate forms of albums. One of the victims of this transition was the elimination of the single album or EP. By the end of the '90s, the full-length CD was the only way to purchase music, and, as album prices soared to a peak of $18.99 per album, there were no inexpensive options when it came to buying music and no way to get a song without purchasing a whole album. Consumers frequently complained about being trapped into buying a full album simply to gain access to one or two songs they were interested in. This was the state of the

---

7 RCA Manufacturing Company, Inc. vs Paul Whiteman, et al.
SDNY (7-25-1939) ¤ 28 F.Supp.787, 43 USPQ 114, reversed by:CCA 2nd Cir. (7-25-1940) ¤ 114 F.2d 86, 46 USPQ 324, cert. denied 311 U.S. 712, 61 S.Ct. 394, 85 L.Ed. 463 (1940).

music marketplace when digital downloads via peer-to-peer networks first emerged.

Napster was launched in summer 1999 by Shawn Fanning, Sean Parker, and John Fanning. People were already sharing files over the Internet, but the technology at the time was unreliable and songs were difficult to find. The goal of Napster was not to invent the process of file sharing—that had already happened—it was to make it easier and more efficient. Once that had been achieved, the site spread like wildfire through college communities and eventually to millions of users worldwide. Faced with the options of paying nearly twenty dollars for an album featuring maybe one song they liked or downloading as many songs as they wanted for free, most people were decided that they liked the sound of the latter more than the former. Not far behind, of course, were the lawsuits that would characterize the next several years of record company policy as well as efforts by record companies to prevent consumers from uploading their CDs to computers. There had been a brief window where the music industry could have approached those who were downloading music and made it clear that they understood the conundrum facing young people who didn't have a lot of money to spend on music and didn't feel like taking a twenty-dollar gamble every time they bought an album. Instead, they immediately went on the defensive and ended up alienating consumers and even some of their artists in what was one of the most highly publicized and written-about incidents of trying to shut the barn door after the horse had already escaped.

In April 2003 Apple Inc. launched the iTunes music store. Within its first week of existence, it counted over a million sales of legal downloads. While it wasn't the end for illegal downloading by a long shot, it was the first legal downloading option that gained widespread appeal and acceptance from the record industry. However, it's hard to tell if the appeal of iTunes was because people were looking for a legal way to do what they had been doing illegally for so long or because people needed iTunes to use the iPod, which came out that same year. Suddenly, average music fans could carry an entire CD collection around in their pocket and easily search for specific songs or artists that they wanted to listen to. Now, the iPod wasn't particularly picky about where you got the music files you were loading onto it, so you could take your entire illicit MP3 collection, transfer it into iTunes, and then put the music on your iPod and never pay a dime for any actual music. But music on iTunes had the benefit of a guaranteed quality level, and you didn't run any risk of downloading a corrupted file or even one that had just been labeled incorrectly. It made downloading safe for people who were skeptical of the Wild-West feel of the file-sharing sites and resolved any issue of questionable legality. One of the more remarkable things about iTunes is how quickly they were able to get access to the catalogs of major record labels, but by the time Steve Jobs announced his plans to the heads of the labels he approached, he knew he had them over a barrel. The first few attempts at digital distribution weren't putting up the kind of numbers the labels had hoped for, and iTunes at least had the iPod in its favor right out of the gate. The 30-percent cut that Jobs stipulated on sales was high, but something the labels were willing to pay.

The most shocking thing about the digital revolution in music is how quickly it happened. Reading the above, you can see that there were less than four years between the launch of Napster and the launch of iTunes. Napster got people used to the idea of downloading music rather than buying a CD, and iTunes gave them a way to buy that music (or upload it from their existing CDs) in a safe, legal way. Not that iTunes caused everyone to suddenly abandon downloading music and begin purchasing it; as the saying goes, why buy the cow if you can get the milk for free? The RIAA campaign against illegal downloading seemed only to incite a certain portion of consumers to download more as a protest against what they saw as unfair persecution of music fans. The RIAA was also able to get many colleges and universities to begin monitoring student Internet usage for illegal downloading, since they had previously been hotbeds of illegal downloading. Students found to be using peer-to-peer networks or torrent sites would usually have their Internet privileges revoked temporarily and then permanently if they were found to be downloading illegally. The RIAA also began offering a sort of plea deal to those who were identified as illegal downloaders that would allow them to pay less in fines and avoid a costly court case. While this was going on, sites hosting illegal activity were still being taken to court by the RIAA in an effort to stop the practice of illegal downloading by cutting off the means to do it.

Many chide the music industry for what is perceived as foot-dragging when it came to adopting digital distribution technology, and there was absolutely a huge amount of arrogance in the way the industry ignored the largest technological development of the '90s and persisted in pushing CDs with ever-increasing prices. However, there were also legal hurdles to overcome; many artist contracts hadn't been written to accommodate digital distribution, since they had been written in a time when the concept of distribution that didn't involve a physical product was unthinkable. Since then, most contracts have been written or amended to include all current distribution methods, followed by some vague language referring to any future method of distribution that will also be covered by the contract. While the labels were able to renegotiate almost all those contracts to account for digital distribution, they didn't have the power to begin selling mp3s immediately. Looking back, some people have questioned why the labels didn't take some of the deals or arrangements that were proposed to them by Sean Parker as the Napster lawsuits were under way, and the issue with contracts is a significant factor.

The other significant difference between the switch to digital and all previous format changes is that changing to digital didn't require people to purchase their entire music collection over again, since computers allowed people to rip their physical CDs directly onto the computer. This was excellent for consumers but bad news for record companies who tended to rely on the added income from people repurchasing music when format changes occurred, even as they railed against them and held out making the change themselves as long as possible. There was no huge drop-off in sales when records switched to tapes and tapes to CDs, because each time people not only were buying new albums in the new format, but also, once consumers completely adopted the new format, they had the choice between keeping around two music systems or repurchasing music. There weren't any other options. With the switch to digital, no one had to re-buy music they already owned as long as it was on a CD. The introduction of technology that would prevent consumers from ripping CDs to their computers was first met with outrage and then derision, as one form of the protection was famously defeated by the high-tech method of scribbling on the silver side of the CD with a marker.

Music subscription services were one of the first options tried by the music industry post-Napster. Many of the early subscription services (including Napster itself after they reinvented themselves in law-abiding fashion) failed. The reasons varied, but one of the more constant refrains was that these services just lacked the variety and volume of songs that the file-sharing networks provided. It was a reasonable complaint; in the early years of subscription services, many big artists didn't have their catalogues available for listening. Over time, though, subscription services have become more popular as their catalogues expanded, and the options for how to access them grew to include smartphones, most of which can be plugged into a car's stereo system or home entertainment unit for listening beyond a computer. One of the bigger arguments that has emerged with regard to subscription services is whether they pay out enough to make them worthwhile for artists, and for independent artist the question is even harder; if you know you're not going to earn more than a few dollars from a subscription service per year, but having your music available on it may gain you new listeners, is it ultimately worth having your music listed? Obviously, each artist is going to have to answer that question for themselves, based on individual goals and services desired from a subscription service.

There are many who are looking at cloud-based music services as being the next big thing to hit the market. This probably has something to do with the fact that in 2010, Google made some very quiet moves toward a cloud-based music service that they would begin offering users along the lines of their cloud-based Google Docs service. *Cloud-based services*, for those of you who may not be familiar with the term, are simply a way of storing music, documents, photos, or any other sort of digital information on a remote server that you can then access from anywhere you have Internet service. They've already been in use through services like Apple's Mobile Me[8] and Digital Dropbox, which gave users a name and password that they could then use to log in to their storage space and use files, even if they weren't at the computer those files were originally stored on. It's an extremely useful tool for people who may do work on more than one computer on a regular basis (which, at this point, is nearly everyone who works with computers) and for people with smartphones, since a cloud-based service means you don't have to have all those files stored on your phone in order to access them anytime you might need to. Some music services have already dipped a toe into the cloud-based field; Spotify offers its premium users the ability to create playlists that can then be accessed from other Internet-enabled devices or on their home computer, even when the computer is not connected to the Internet. The service sits somewhere between transmission and cloud.

Given the rate of change in the digital realm, it seems foolish to make predictions about the future since they're equally likely to be obsolete as they are to be deemed completely impossible. What we're moving towards seems to be personalized music collections available anywhere the user has Internet access to either music they've purchased or a streaming service. We've gone from a Walkman that would carry one tape, to the Discman that carried a CD, to the iPod that carried thousands of songs, and next will likely be a cloud system that will allow users to potentially have millions of

---

8 Which was discontinued once Apple launched iCloud, another cloud-based service.

songs available to them almost anytime and anywhere. From the introduction of the phonograph to today, the way we listen to music has changed in ways that were unimaginable, and the largest leap has happened since the year 2000, as the necessity for a physical copy of music has been eliminated by digital music.

Throughout the years that music has been sold directly to consumers, from the days of sheet music up until now, the goal has been the same: create music that people want to hear and find ways to profit from that. What has changed is the barriers to distribution that once existed. The digital revolution that began in the '90s with the development of the Internet for home use and continued to roll into the 2000s with the introduction of broadband connections and huge leaps forward in data storage technology have completely changed the opportunities available to artists who want to distribute their music.

CHAPTER 3:

HOW I LEARNED TO STOP WORRYING AND LOVE THE INTERNET

The first and most important thing to keep in mind about the Internet is this: it's not going away. That cat is out of the bag, and yes, it does mean that there are people who will download your music for free without feeling guilty. In fact, many of them will expect that privilege as a matter of course. I won't argue that it's fair, or right, or something we should be excited about, but it's best to just get it out of the way that it's true and not waste time talking about why it shouldn't be true. By and large this is more a problem for major record labels with acts that people are deliberately seeking out on the Internet than independent bands still trying to attract a following. There are many independent artists who will give music away just to gain listeners who will then purchase tickets to shows and other merchandise that are going to be larger moneymakers than album royalties. However, that isn't an attitude shared by all artists and the desire to be compensated for your work isn't something anyone should demonize. With the one large downside of the possibility of illegal downloading, there's a lot of good that skillful use of the Internet can do for independent artists and their fans, and that's what I'd rather talk about.

Independents actually have far less to fear and far more to love about the Internet than they might think. For big artists, the ones signed to major labels especially, the fear of their album leaking to the Internet is constant and well founded. The release of super group The Throne's album Watch the Throne was notable for several reasons, but the lack of pre-release Internet leaks was a big one. The details of the hard drives equipped with fingerprint scans held under lock and key and mandatory in person playback sessions, though, illustrate how hard it can be to keep information private when you've got whole teams of people passing it around.[9] There have been a few cases where artists have managed to peak on the basis of leaked tracks before an album was even available for purchase, which is partially the fault of online leaks and partially the fault of a certain kind of fan culture that seems to revolve around finding new bands or songs that are farther and farther removed from whatever passes for 'mainstream' at that particular moment. There's dispute over whether artists and record companies orchestrate these leaks or not, with some saying that it's done to drum up publicity for the new album and others pointing out that not only is the album and/or songs available for free so it doesn't financially benefit anyone but it also means that the version of the song out that people are listening to is one that hasn't been fully mastered yet. As in, a song that is not up to the usual standards of the artist.

For those that do fall victim to Internet piracy, reactions are mixed. Some artists will believe that any exposure is beneficial to their career and won't take steps to prevent their music from being pirated. Some big name artists have actually encouraged fans to pirate their music when they felt that their labels weren't pricing their albums fairly (Nine Inch Nails) or

---

9 *Billboard*, "Protecting The Throne: How Jay-Z & Kanye Beat the Leaks" Stephen J. Horowitz, August 15th, 2011.

when the label hadn't made their music available in certain markets where people wanted to buy it (Skrillex). There's also been something of a public push for artists to allow their music to be available for free anywhere in the world. This is a decision artists have to make individually and it does not speak ill of you as an artist to say that you want to be compensated for your work. As great as it may be to know that there are over fifty thousand people downloading your song through sites offering torrents[10] or other file-sharing services, it's significantly less satisfying to know that those numbers aren't going to have an effect on your bank account. If you do find that your songs are available on file-sharing sites without your permission, there are steps you can take to get them taken down.

On January 20th, 2012, the owner of Brooklyn's Projeckt Records, Sam Rosenthal, did an interview with *Digital Music News* in which he detailed the process of getting songs removed from file sharing sites, and recommended that artists or independent labels make it part of their weekly schedule. The process sounds simple (find illegal content, file a "takedown notice," the site takes the file down) but Rosenthal goes into detail regarding each step that makes it clear that it is rarely straightforward or even effective. It's worth reading the entire interview, but some of the high points are listed below:

1. Use FilesTube to search for infringing content. This is a search engine that looks into "locker" file-sharing sites. Under each file it finds will be a download button. Once you click on that, you'll be able to see a white box with "direct links," which are what you copy to the e-mail message you're going to send with the takedown notice.

2. Set up a Google alert with your band name and most recent album or single name that will e-mail you once a day with any hits for the

---

10 A file format that allows for downloading very large media files relatively quickly.

names. This should help you find infringing content more easily, and it can also help you find legitimate mentions as well.

3. Once you have the links, you can e-mail the sites to alert them to illegal uploads of the music and demand that those links be removed. Some sites will have a specific set of "takedown instructions" but Rosenthal encourages you to e-mail them directly since they will take down anything that gets a complaint. He also says he copies all the links to one e-mail that he sends to all file sharing sites rather than parsing out individual links to send to specific sites, but you can handle that differently if you want.

4. Use a statement like this in the e-mail: "Under penalty of perjury, I am the owner of the copyrighted works listed below. I ask for the immediate removal of all these files from your site. These are illegal infringements, uploaded without my permission. Please remove them and e-mail a confirmation." Include your name, band name, and contact information and then the links.[11]

Some people characterize independent artists or labels who issue takedown notices and discourage illegal file-sharing as being hostile to their fans. I don't believe this is the case, but reactions are going to be mixed, depending on the viewpoint of the person speaking. Whether you encourage file sharing or not, make your position clear to your fans on your website, Facebook page, or wherever it is you find they're connecting with you.

One of the most obvious resources available for independent artists online is access to companies that can manufacture and distribute your album via online stores and give you the option of making your album available on iTunes. The move to digital distribution has become the great leveler in terms of giving artists power, since once upon a time it was virtually impossible to make your music available without distribution support.

---

11 The direct link to this article is http://digitalmusicnews.com/permalink/2012/12012 0megasupport

Once CDs hit the market, you could make your own or pay a company to manufacture a run for you, but you still had to get them out there on your own, and putting CDs in the hands of anyone you didn't interact with directly was almost impossible. With digital distribution, you can release your music to the world in less time than it takes to get a suit dry-cleaned and, in some cases, for less outlay on your part. With some services, you don't even have to bother with a whole album, since they have options available for singles or EP-style releases with only a few songs. Unless you've got a fantastic artistic reason to release a full album, it's worth looking into putting your strongest single out first to test the waters before committing to recording and mastering a whole ten to twelve songs. What follows is a partial list of services that exist both in the US and abroad to help musicians deliver their music to digital distributors and an analysis of what services they offer for what pricing. Some services take no money up front and rely entirely on a percentage of money earned from digital sales; others will promise you 100 percent of net royalties (royalties minus the cut from the distributor) but ask for an up-front fee based on what you're distributing. It's up to each artist or band to decide which approach is the one that's right for them, but hopefully this list can give you some insight into what your options are.

CDBaby was launched in 1999 with the goal of giving musicians direct access to distribution without the middleman of a record label or distribution company. The site will ship CDs from their own warehouse and offers digital downloads through their website as well as through retailers like iTunes. CDBaby has expanded their options to involve more than just CDs and downloads, though; they've added download cards that contain codes that will let fans download songs or full albums, giving artists a cheaper way to sell albums directly to fans or give out their information along with a code for a download to prospective clients without having to carry around a bag full of CDs. You'll also be able to track how many people actually download from the card, which you obviously can't do with CDs. CDBaby also provides artists with the information on people who buy their CDs through the CDBaby website, unless the customers specifically opt out. This can be great information for artists who are to the point where they're looking into planning a tour or who are organized enough to have a regular newsletter of some kind that they send out to fans to keep them updated on future shows, new releases, and so on.

CDBaby operates on a money-up-front structure, with different price rates for different services. Uploading an album for digital distribution and streaming through iTunes, Amazon MP3, Rhapsody, Napster, eMusic, MOG, Spotify, and Verizon costs a fixed amount rather than a yearly fee. They also keep 9 percent of net earnings; that is, earnings once the fee from those digital distributors or streaming services has been deducted. The same cut is put on singles, though the rate to upload singles to those distributors is much less than the album rate, so it's worthwhile to do a little math to see if the number of songs you have would be better served by the album or single pricing structure. There are some discounts if you plan to submit multiple singles or albums at the same time, so make sure to poke around in the "Submission Credits" section before you commit to a pricing structure if you've got multiple songs or albums you're interested in selling through their service.

CDBaby also offers several services that aren't directly music-related, like selling credit-card swipers, so you can accept credit-card transactions at your gigs, barcodes so you can accurately track all sales of your physical CDs no matter what outlets they go through, and web hosting services. This makes it a great one-stop shop if you've got a bit of money to throw around and prefer to have all of these services consolidated under one account, though for many of these components you can find better pricing elsewhere. For example, they sell a credit-card swiper for thirty dollars plus shipping and handling and keep 9 percent of sales plus 3.8 percent to cover credit-card fees. Also, it's an old-style swiper that works with carbon sales slips rather than on a digital basis. You have to mail the slips in, and

CDBaby will account to you on a weekly basis. If you've got a smartphone or an iPad, you can use the Square credit card reader, which is free, with a free app, and that company charges a flat 2.75 percent per swipe for all credit cards. If you have to enter a card number manually, the charge goes up to 3.5 percent plus a fifteen-cent fee, but that's still coming in way below the service CDBaby offers. Also, Square will directly deposit to your bank account. I'm not saying this as a commercial for Square, but to point out that looking around and comparing pricing structures for these services can take some time but save you a lot of money in the long run. There are several different companies offering apps and hardware that can turn smartphones into credit-card readers or virtual cash registers, so see which might be best for you.

Founded in 2005, TuneCore operates much the same way as CDBaby when it comes to artists uploading their own songs and artwork but differently in that TuneCore's primary goal is not creating physical albums but rather acting as a way for artists to make their album available for worldwide digital distribution whether or not they have a physical album available. As opposed to CDBaby, TuneCore's pricing structure is a monthly fee[12] rather than an up-front payment, and they take no percentage of your sales. They also offer the ability to distribute ringtones and the chance to make your song available for download on the game Rock Band, which are things that CDBaby doesn't offer. TuneCore's services also include partnering with Universal Music Group to help get their artists licensing deals and physical distribution to Guitar Center stores for "qualifying artists." They also provide free digital cover art and UPCs, though perhaps it would be more accurate to say that those services are included in what you pay for rather than "free." Like with CDBaby, there's a volume pricing option available, so be sure to look into that if you think it would apply.

---

12 I'm not including specific numbers here in case the fees change between the time I'm writing this and the time you're reading it. I'd rather be vague than give inaccurate information.

While it may seem silly to make CDs in this day and age, Nielsen Soundscan revealed that in 2011 two-thirds of the albums purchased in the US were in CD format[13]. Digital album sales are still gaining in the music marketplace, and CD sales are falling overall, but if you've got a local independent record store, coffee shop, or other retail location that would be willing to stock your CDs and sell them, it can be worth the time and effort to make CDs available for impulse purchasers. This is another area where having a healthy social-media presence can help, since you can poll your fans to find out how and where they typically buy music, and figure out how to target them and other fans like them in order to dedicate your efforts to the distribution method most likely to win you new fans and (hopefully) make you money.

Aside from TuneCore and CDBaby, there are other online distribution services that operate in other ways than the pay-per-album model both of the above offer. Record Union allows you to list music for free (as long as you have a UPC code, though they also sell those for ten dollars if you don't) but will take the first five dollars annually from releases that are generating money and 15 percent of sales income. There are other US-based services out there if you want to do your research; CDBaby and TuneCore are the largest and as such are probably not the cheapest. As the largest of these services, though, they offer more name recognition and business partnerships to first time artists that can be worth the extra cost.

It's not just the US where these services can be found; there are also a number of companies based in the UK and Europe that offer similar services. DittoMusic will put an album or single on iTunes for free and offers free ringtone service but leverages fees once you start adding in other distributors like Amazon or Spotify. DittoMusic offers musicians 100 percent of the net proceeds from distributors though, as opposed to most sites that

---

13   Digital Music New, "Two Thirds of All Albums Purchased In the US Are Still CD", Wednesday, January 4th, 2012. "http://www.digitalmusicnews.com/permalink/2012/120104twothirds"

take a percentage of sales. AWAL charges no up-front fees and works on a rolling thirty-day term for agreements but takes a 15 percent commission from music sold. The State 51 Conspiracy also provides digital distribution, but their website was not particularly forthcoming with information regarding their pricing structures or what kind of commissions they take from sales. Emu Bands offers the standard fee per album or single model and charges no annual fees and doesn't take a cut of royalties earned from sales. They also offer registration with Shazam and Gracenote for additional fees. Zimbalam, which is based out of Paris, also offers a flat-fee model for sign-up and takes a 10 percent commission. They also allow users to specify which stores or services the artist wants to make their music available on after they sign up. Spain-based La Cúpula charges 0.75€ per track to list music, rather than standard album or single fees, and also guarantees 100 percent of royalties will be returned to the artist. While these services may not seem like something a fledgling artist necessarily needs, they're worth keeping in mind for their pricing options, since most of them offer worldwide listings on iTunes and all other international services, so the fact that they're not US-based would not have an impact on how your music appeared on those services. The accounting, though, might get a little difficult at times.

A more direct method of making your music available for purchase has emerged with the recently launched Google Music, which subsequently became known as Google Play. While it can be a bit tricky to find,[14] there is a way for artists to put their music on Google Play on their own for a twenty-five-dollar one-time set-up fee. This gives you the right to upload unlimited albums, tracks, and make changes anytime you like without an annual fee. Google keeps a 30 percent commission on all sales through their market, but that's a standard 30 percent no

---

14 Go to the Android Market/Google music market page and scroll all the way to the bottom. On the same line as the 2011 Google copyright notice, there's a small link that says "artists" that takes you to the page that will let you sign up.

matter how you price your music. Google also gives you the option to make certain tracks album only, which is lacking in many of the other sites that let artists upload their work to iTunes or other digital retailers. Earnings are paid out monthly, rather than once artists hit a set dollar amount or on a quarterly basis, and since the money doesn't pass through an intermediary, it seems likely artists could get paid faster this way than through other services. If you've set up a YouTube partner account, you can link it to your Google Play artist page, and fans can buy your music directly through the YouTube page. And for artists using the Artist Hub to upload their music directly, Google has a "Magnified Artists by Google Play" program to help promote the efforts of independent artists that they pick through "a combination of editorial input, sales performances, shares on Google+ and other fan engagement data." Obviously there are downfalls; right now the service is available only for US-based artists, and since Google Play for music is still in its infancy, it's impossible to say if selling your music there will make you any money at all. For groups that have built a fan base that's just this side of tech savvy and that would be willing to follow them to a new service, it's something I'd recommend looking at, just because of the level of control and relatively cheap fee structure they have in place.

One of the things to watch with the Google/Android music market is how much it influences other industry leaders in the digital-music marketplace. When Google announced their Google Music cloud service, iTunes wasn't far behind in developing their own plan for a cloud service. Now we have both Google Music and iTunes Match. Up until now, the only option artists have had to get their music on iTunes was working through intermediary services like the ones listed previously. If iTunes decides to compete with the model set by Google, where artists can upload their own music and get paid directly, then it could put a lot of different digital-music aggregators out of business but also give artists more direct control of what music they make available to digital retailers and how.

Google isn't the first service to give musicians direct access to distribution channels; Amazon's CreateSpace has a music division that gives artists the ability to have CDs made on demand (when someone orders one rather than ordering stock that may or may not sell) and the ability to make their music available through Amazon's MP3 service. The service isn't exactly up-front about the costs involved, though they do promise no set-up fees, and that you will earn royalties on every sale, though not exactly what percentage of those royalties will go to you versus CreateSpace. If you're looking to manufacture physical CDs, there's also a considerable lead time that you need to take into account after you send in your mastered recordings and artwork. The biggest advantage of CreateSpace over something like CD Baby is that you don't have to preorder inventory and pay up front, so if your fan base prefers to buy CDs rather than digital downloads (older demographics, typically) this may be a better option for making a physical product available in a cost-effective and easily purchasable way.

If you do sign up with a distributor service, be sure you read through every inch of what you're signing up for, although even that won't always keep you completely informed of what will be done with your music. In April 2012, TechDirt did a report on an incident where a songwriter, John Boydston, had an infringement claim filed against him on his own song by Rumblefish. He filed a dispute and was told that it would be processed, but that in the meantime any ads appearing on his video would monetarily benefit Rumblefish rather than the songwriter. So what had happened? The band (Daddy A Go Go) had signed up with CDBaby for online distribution. In addition to the usual outlets like iTunes, Amazon, and streaming services, CDBaby also sent their music along to Rumblefish, which is supposed to help songwriters get their music licensed for television, movies, commercials, and so on. Rumblefish then entered the band's music into their YouTube ContentID system, so that when the song was detected on YouTube, they would send the income the videos generated back to Rumblefish, no matter who uploaded them. None of this was explicitly spelled out on CDBaby's website, so it came as something of a shock to the band and probably to other bands who read about the incident. In the wake of this incident, Boydston decided to uncheck the box that allowed Rumblefish access to his music. If you decide to sign up with an aggregator service like CDBaby or TuneCore (or any other one), it would be better if you checked only the boxes for the services that you know for sure what they'll do with your music. Services like Rumblefish that offer to help promote your music for licensing sound attractive, but since many music supervisors will conduct their own music searches or work through recommendations, it's questionable how much they can help.

Any financial arrangement to digitally distribute music should be something the band or artist revisits periodically to make sure the arrangement still makes sense for them financially and that they aren't wasting money on services they don't need or that aren't earning them any money. And if you've got a little time and programming know-how, there is the option of selling your music entirely independently through your own website, if you can make MP3s and have a way of getting them to fans. You'll have a smaller reach through your own website rather than through a large digital retailer like iTunes or Amazon, but you'll keep 100 percent of the profits and have full control over things like price points or if you choose to make songs available only for a limited time.

A 2011 breakdown from the UK by label group BPI showed that 68 percent of albums purchased in the last year were physical. Unfortunately, without a better analysis of those numbers, it's difficult to say if that's because people prefer to buy physical rather than digital, or because physical albums were more convenient to purchase. If the reason that many physical albums were sold is because they were purchased as impulse items at a mega-mart, that's not going to help an independent artist whose albums aren't going to go on sale at the local Target,[15] even if you create a physical CD. The choice of whether or not to create a physical album should be

---

15 Or Tesco, in keeping with the data being from the UK.

based on what your fans are most interested in rather than on generalized statistics, numbers, or advice. Some artists do sell a lot of physical albums, even when they're available only through digital distributors and require shipping and all the other inconveniences that come with that. Some artists live with boxes of unsold albums hanging around their closet forever. The biggest question in the digital versus physical argument for independent artists is about the money involved. While there are fees associated with most digital distribution services offered through these aggregators, those costs are relatively low if you've already got the sound files in hand. Creating a CD and ordering a stock of them does require you to pay money up front for manufacturing and shipping those CDs. Having your music available digitally should be your first step, and, as you interact with your fans and play shows, you can discern whether it would be to your advantage to have a physical product to sell.

For those worried about having a physical product available for live shows or meeting people that you would want to give your album to in person, the modern era has offered a sort of workaround for the slightly tech-savvy. QR codes are easy to create with free software or apps and link back to URLs, applications, or even downloads. Putting a QR code that leads to your band's website where your album is for sale digitally, or one that lets someone download your single to their phone instantly, can help bridge the gap between wanting to have product on hand immediately without the expense of manufacturing CDs and the difficulty of carrying them around with you everywhere.

The business of selling music either digitally or in physical form through digital retailers is the least of the opportunities the Internet affords artists. While incredibly useful, these services only scratch the surface of the ways that artists can use the Internet to build a fan base and spread their music across the country or across the world. In order to grasp just how much can happen on the Internet below the radar of major labels, one can look at the career of Lily Allen. In 2005 Allen posted demos from the recording sessions for her debut album *Alright, Still* on MySpace and began attracting thousands of listeners. The album was rushed into production, but since Allen's MySpace page was established by her rather than by her label, the number of fans she had already accumulated was something of a shock. Allen was selling out clubs in the US before the album was released stateside. In fact, by the time her album was released in the US, in 2007, Allen had already played a sold-out tour in North America. Allen's record hadn't even been on her label's release schedule before her songs took MySpace by storm, and it's not hard to come to the conclusion that the popularity Allen found through the Internet kept her label from quietly releasing her album only to sweep it under the rug.[16] Many artists over the decades have watched labels that had been enthusiastic quickly lose interest in their projects and meet only the bare contractual minimums before letting the contract lapse. This can change with the Internet, although more likely artists will just have to sign contracts that prohibit releasing material before the record labels do. The instant feedback you gain from the Internet can be a boon to bands that aren't on a label, though, as they let you gauge your audience and their interests on a day-to-day, if not an hour-to-hour, basis.

More recently the power of the Internet has been critical in the spread of electronic dance music, a genre that doesn't lend itself easily to traditional album-style releases. Artists like Diplo, Skrillex, Swedish House Mafia, DeadMau5, and others are artists whose style of composition is less defined by tracks and recordings than it is by a free-form, open-ended stream of sound that can change based on the venue, the fans, or the artist's mood that particular evening. While some of these artists have released proper albums, all of them built buzz through online followings before the mainstream music business began to pay serious attention. The Ultra festival in Miami, heavily devoted to electronic dance music, has a history of selling out months in advance. The performance of these electronic artists at other festivals like Coachella has overwhelmed venues and shocked organizers.

---

16 *Wired*, Kot, pg. 211-213.

It's a trend that hasn't hit most radio stations, that lives almost entirely at live shows, and is spread through word of mouth, largely through the Internet. It's a new form of underground music, and as kids grow up with things like Facebook and YouTube as a fact of life, it stands to reason that these outlets are going to become primary destinations for music discovery.

One of the sites that's very useful for bands looking to establish a professional-looking Internet presence and also gives you the ability to track data about your fans and integrate with Facebook is Bandcamp. They give you statistics on who is linking back to you, which tracks are most popular, when people are downloading, what search terms are leading back to your site, and other information that can help you better define and cater to your audience. Bandcamp also offers a pre-search-engine optimized site, which means that your site on Bandcamp.com will be a higher hit in Google than third-party sites that may list information on your band without your permission as a way to gain traffic. You can distribute your music in digital download format directly through Bandcamp via a Bandcamp-hosted site or on a custom Bandcamp page featuring downloads. You get to name your own price and get a certain amount of free downloads allocated automatically each month, with the option to buy more if you want to give out more. There's also the chance to generate discount codes for purchases, in case you want to run special sales for fans at different times. They charge no up-front fees and simply take a percentage of sales: 15 percent on the first $5,000 USD worth of sales and 10 percent after that on products up to $100. Now, that's a cut on all sales, so if you're using your Bandcamp page to sell merchandise other than digital downloads, they'll be getting a cut of that too. Bandcamp also doesn't help you create merchandise, so what you can sell on the site will be limited only by what you can afford to have made up.

The two most valuable things that Bandcamp helps you with are (1) quickly and easily establishing a professional Internet presence and (2) Facebook integration, which allows you to capture fans where they find you instead of having to redirect them to another site to purchase your album or other merchandise. Going through an established site also helps fans feel better about purchasing things from your store. Unlike TuneCore and CDBaby, they don't offer the ability to get music on iTunes or create a physical CD, but you can get yourself up and rolling without any out-of-pocket expenses, and once you see if your music is moving or where your fans are, you can make the call on whether to spend the money to get your music on iTunes or other digital distribution services.

For those looking for resources online that focus more on the creative process than sales and distribution, the Internet can offer countless ways to connect with other artists or people interested in using your music. While I was speaking to Tim Nordwind of OK Go for chapter four, he talked about this as something he sees happening with the Internet that's beneficial for young artists. "There's places that people go to collaborate on music, which I think is cool. Like Indaba [Music] where people go to post music for other people to work on. So you're getting collaborations between people in like, Iowa and somewhere in Europe or in South America or something like that. You have people all over the world working on music together, which I think is very cool from a creative point of view." Other sites with similar features include Kompoz, MyOnlineBand, and MusiciansCollaboration. com. If you're interested in working this way, give each site a visit and see what they have to offer, then figure out which is the best fit for your needs.

The services I've highlighted in this chapter are all extremely worthy of attention. However, because of the nature of the Internet, there are new services springing up every day, and unless I wanted to devote an entire book to various websites and what they offer for your band, I'm going to be leaving some things out. If you're looking for services not listed here or are just interested in comparing what's out there, the website Sell Your Band (SellYourBand.com) compiles many different sites and services that are specific to musicians just starting out. Everything from getting a web page up and running to developing mobile apps for iPhones or Androids can be found here. Most of the sites that Sell Your Band points to still require you to do most of the work, but it's a good jumping-off point that keeps you from sitting around attempting to find things on your own with Google. Every band's needs are going to be different, but be grateful that the Internet was developed to create exactly the thing you need before you know you need it, or at the very least to provide you with the tools to make it yourself. It really is the greatest thing that's ever happened in terms of equalizing access to services and information for musicians and the rest of the world.

The largest Internet pitfall is also the most obvious: putting your music on the Internet makes it available for piracy. Realistically, if you intend to release your music to the public, there's no way to guard against it ending up available for illegal downloading or torrents, so the question is less about what you're going to do to keep your music from getting out of your hands and more about what are you going to do with people who find your music no matter what the avenue they come by. Do you have a well-organized website with clear information about your band and upcoming performances, with links to purchase tickets either on your own or through a service? Do you have a Facebook page people can join or a Twitter feed that will send out announcements about shows and upcoming projects? Do you have a YouTube channel with music videos that fans can watch to see your band in action? Before putting your music online, it's best to look at all these factors, so that even if you can't control how people come by your music, you can ensure that, when they look for more information on you, the information is clear and easy to find. Even if someone can download a song without your earning anything from it, it's still impossible to download a T-shirt, and an entertaining and energetic live show can't be replicated online.

Distribution used to be the biggest hurdle for a band, and having distribution showed that either someone believed in you enough to invest the money to print your album, or that you had some serious cash of your own to pay to get your own recordings pressed. Now almost anyone with an Internet connection and a decent microphone can record work and get it on the Internet. You need to find a new way to distinguish yourself from all the other artists in the marketplace, a way to get people to pay attention to you as opposed to all the other acts out there who also have music on YouTube, iTunes, Spotify, or any other service. And once you get people to pay attention to you, you have to hold their attention and give them a good reason to stay interested and engaged in what you have to offer. If people like you, they'll talk about you, and you can build your audience one fan at a time. Besides, it is incredible to realize the scope of change the Internet has had on the music industry. As Tim Nordwind put it, "There's certainly all sorts of ways to find band members online, make music online, distribute it online, and raise the money you want to make the project online. It's kind of amazing to do all that from your desk if you want to."

CHAPTER 4:

CASE STUDY: OK GO PRESENTS FIFTY WAYS TO LEAVE YOUR LABEL

A n excellent example of a band that uses the Internet to their advantage on a regular basis is OK Go. Whether you want to talk about viral videos, social media presence, an engaged online fan base, or simply a smartly designed and easy-to-navigate website, OK Go has it all going for them. They've been in the business since the release of their first self-titled album in 2002, and in 2010 they announced that they would be leaving their record label. There were a lot of factors that went into this decision, and several of them revolved around the band's use of and belief in the Internet as a powerful tool for good rather than a way to make money. Since leaving their label, OK Go has continued to use the Internet as their primary means of reaching new and current fans.

OK Go was a band that didn't have a huge amount of success at the beginning of their career. While their first single, "Get Over It," off their self-titled debut, earned a few placements in video games and movies, it wasn't a hit. That all changed one fateful afternoon in the spring 2005, when the band took to lead singer Damien Kulash's backyard and performed a dance routine choreographed by Kulash's sister, Trish Sie, to "A Million Ways," a song that would be included on their upcoming album *Oh No*. The video became a quiet hit and inspired many fans to learn the dance and upload their own attempts at the choreography to YouTube. The band performed the dance at concerts and even started a contest where fans could win the chance to perform the "Million Ways" dance with the band at a future concert. And if OK Go had stopped there, it would still be commendable that they used YouTube to attract attention to themselves and build their fan base. But they weren't done—not by a long shot.

On July 31, 2006, the video for "Here It Goes Again" featured OK Go performing choreography by Trish Sie on a series of treadmills. Shot in one continuous take, the video took the Internet by storm as it was passed around, embedded, and linked to by thousands of fans and dozens of websites. Within a week the video had rocketed to one million YouTube views. The band was invited to perform the dance live at the VMAs which they managed to do without injury to themselves or spectators. It was a phenomenon, and introduced millions of people to OK Go even if most of them only knew them as the band in the treadmill video. Eventually, they reached the pinnacle of American culture when the video was spoofed on "The Simpsons." They changed their career, and a lot of peoples' ideas about what a music video could or should be.

While this may all seem to be a product of dumb luck, OK Go's relationship with the Internet goes well beyond goofy dancing videos. Kulash testified in front of the House Judiciary Committee's Anti-Trust Task Force in favor of Internet neutrality in March 2008. At that hearing, which came after the success of "Here It Goes Again," Kulash emphasized the boost the Internet had given the band: "Whether you think our videos are brilliant or gimmicky—I'd be the first to say they're a little of both—they've done more to promote our music to an audience around the world than anything else we or our label has produced.... We believe the videos were so loved because they came directly from us. There was no one telling us what we could or couldn't do, no middlemen or marketers, and we didn't have to sell a committee of gatekeepers on our idea before we could take it to our fans. Our success couldn't have happened in the pay-to-play music industry of ten years ago, or in a world without an open, unbiased, and unfettered Internet." While the plan for "A Million Ways" hadn't been millions of views and worldwide exposure, when it did accomplish this, the band was able to take that moment and build on it, thanks to the immediacy of the Internet and the availability of technology that let them create and upload videos easily. This wasn't a marketing plan, it wasn't focus-grouped, and there wasn't a committee behind it deciding how these videos would help or hurt the band's "image." These were projects that OK Go themselves conceptualized and realized independent of their label or any other outside input, and none of it could have happened without the Internet and the free and easy exchange of information it offered. These experiences laid the groundwork for the next stage of their career.

In 2010 the relationship between the band and their label, EMI, finally came to a boiling point over allowing OK Go's videos to be embedded on third-party websites. After YouTube began paying fractions of a cent for video plays on YouTube.com but not for plays via embedded videos on external sites, it became industry practice to eliminate the embedding option for all music videos. The dispute began in January 2010, when Kulash took to the forum on OKGo.net to explain why the first video for their single "This Too Shall Pass" couldn't be embedded on external sites. On February 20, an op-ed by Kulash appeared in the *New York Times* further detailing the band's technique of using viral videos to attract fans and their frustration with the label that had hamstrung their efforts in the name of revenue. In what could later be seen as foreshadowing, Kulash wrote, "In these tight times, it's no surprise that EMI is trying to wring revenue out of everything we make, including our videos. But it needs to recognize the basic mechanics of the Internet. Curbing the viral spread of videos isn't benefiting the company's bottom line, or the music it's there to support. The sooner record companies realize this, the better—though I fear it may already be too late." A month later, OK Go would formally leave Capitol/ EMI to form their own label called Paracadute Recordings. Before that, though, the second video for "This Too Shall Pass" hit the Internet—a video that was brilliant in its own right and was the first video made with an outside sponsor in a way that the band would further explore on their own. The band had gotten funding from State Farm Insurance to create a giant Rube Goldberg device with the help of Syyn Labs. The nearly four-minute-long video followed an unbroken string of events leading up to the band getting shot with paint cannons. The video was embedded and relinked to on dozens, if not hundreds, of sites across the Internet, and the view count skyrocketed in the first few days. Following the "This Too Shall Pass" video, OK Go released other videos created through partnerships with Google Chrome ("All Is Not Lost") and, with the financial support of Range Rover, led a parade through downtown Los Angeles with a route plotted out to spell "OK Go" when drawn on a map.

After leaving their label, OK Go began to build a business plan that didn't rely on selling records or royalties from YouTube as a means of survival, and they continued to make music videos that were different, eye-catching, and creative. In an interview with *Billboard* magazine, Kulash and bassist Tim Nordwind discussed the future of Paracadute records, what they were relying on for income, and their goal of developing more creative projects whether or not they had anything to do with music, exactly. The first thing they point out is that if you just want to look at record sales alone, as Kulash points out, that "it takes a lot fewer records sold to pay for our operation to survive than it does to support an international distribution company." They also touched on their concept for sponsorship deals like the one with State Farm that resulted in the "This Too Shall Pass" Rube Goldberg video, with Kulash saying, "The kind [of advertising] that suits us best is good old-fashioned patronage of the arts.... It can associate your brand and your product and the things you do with real awesomeness." They also talked about the fact that their licensing income was more important to them than record sales.

In 2012 the band found a new partner in Chevy and made a video for "Needing/Getting" that featured the band performing the song in a car that interactively "played" a road course of custom-made instruments. The video was a huge investment and took months of work to create, starting with how to create the song using instruments that could be played by a car driving by and then going forward to how to break up the song in the form of a course the car could drive through. While the video was not completed in one take the way some of their more popular videos were, it certainly didn't look like anyone else's music video and earned the band a whole new wave of publicity when it premiered in the pregame coverage of the 2012 Super Bowl. Once again, their video was featured on countless blogs, Tumblrs, Facebook posts, and just about everything in between. OK Go got a new wave of publicity, and Chevy got their car seen by millions of people who were probably only barely aware they were being marketed to—another win-win situation for a band that was increasingly becoming known for things that had very little to do with music.

I was fortunate enough to get the chance to speak with band member Timothy Nordwind about OK Go's history, what their plan was for the foreseeable future, and what he thought of the resources available to new artists today. I first asked how the band approached leaving EMI and creating their independent label, Paracadute. According to Nordwind, "We didn't have like a master plan to leave the label, ever. They funded our band, they kept us on tour a long time and helped us make videos and things like that. But it sort of seemed like towards the end of our years with our label, we started realizing that they sort of have a one-size-fits-all type of method. They get a band, they put you through their system. If you fit with their system then awesome; if you don't, there's a problem. And the basic way that they keep the lights on and keep business going is by selling master recordings, and I think most people who are interested in music at all or in the music business kind of know that sales of music have drastically gone down in the last ten to fifteen years. It seemed sort of obvious to us as we got towards the end that record sales weren't working for us, but we were finding value in a lot of other things that we do, especially like the videos and live shows, and we were being asked to do all sorts of untraditional projects that were creatively appealing and also financially appealing for us, but that didn't necessarily make our label any money, because we weren't selling our song." But of course, they were selling their song in a roundabout way. "It was hard to explain to them that several million views per video, even if it didn't sell the song, it was getting the song out there and it was doing something for our band. And it meant that we were selling more songs than we would have without the successful videos, we were selling more tickets to live shows, we were selling more merchandise. There's things we wouldn't have been able to be a part of if we had only decided to just sell records, and so I'd say after releasing our third record, *Of the Blue Colour of the Sky*, when they had turned off embed-ability for the song "WTF," that was kind of the beginning of the end there. We couldn't understand why they would want to block access to a video that would get the song out there to the world, especially because at that point we were known for our videos, so it was kind of ridiculous to block access to that." This series of events—their viral popularity leading them toward business opportunities that were entirely separate from selling records—is what ended up pushing them over the edge. As Nordwind put it, "We saw that we were going in one direction and they were really going in another. It just doesn't make sense ever, to me, that you would want to make it difficult for people to find your band. So much of this business is just word of mouth or blog love. If you can't pass something around, it becomes more difficult for us to get work."

So now that they've got their own label and can make all of their songs and videos available to be freely embedded across the Internet, what's the next step? "I think the name of the game these days is figuring out alternative methods for distributing and alternative methods for funding. That's something that, as we've developed our own label, the trick has been figuring out if the major label's not going to be funding us, who will? We were lucky enough to find ourselves in a position that after we'd been funded by a major label for ten years, we were in a good position to go out on our own and look for alternative funding and distribution. It's a great method, and it's worked reasonably well for us since we left our label, but it's not necessarily going to work for every band because, like I said, we were able to live off funding from a major label for so many years and we built a grassroots following that we could then take with us off the label, and we were of interest to different people that would sponsor us because of our track record with our videos." Tim also sees this as a growing trend in the music industry, pointing out that "you see all these kinds of untraditional relationships between bands and corporate sponsors that you didn't necessarily see ten to fifteen years ago," which is not unique to OK Go. That's not to say that it was an easy ride the entire time, since the band did have their struggles with the label. Tim says that OK Go wasn't content to sit back and let their label drive their career the way the label saw fit, which led to some issues. "We had to fight harder for the things that we really wanted because we had to get the OK from the label to do all these things. We'd just get in these crazy wrestling matches; to do the tour that we wanted or the video that we wanted or whatever kind of crazy project that we thought was interesting to us, that would be beneficial to us, was always kind of a constant struggle." Given that the timing of these projects (the "A Million Ways" video that started their viral video career came out in early summer 2005 with the infamous treadmills of "Here It Goes Again" hitting YouTube on July 31, 2006) happened to coincide with a merger that ended up with the man who had signed OK Go being dismissed from the newly reorganized Capitol/EMI label, it's easy to see how OK Go might have felt a lack of personal attention under the new leadership.

When I asked Tim about his opinion on major label contracts for young bands, if he thought it was worth it to give up the rights they ask for in exchange for the services they offer, he said, "I guess that's the million-dollar question, and there really is no one right answer that works for everybody. I wish I could just say 'Oh, go the independent route' to give you an easy answer to your question." Ultimately it depends on the band; not every band is going to have the capacity to take themselves from a buzzy independent group to a successful act that can do music full time without the kind of support that a major label offers. The process of doing so is getting easier every day, though, and increasingly bands have the option of obtaining major-label-type support without actually signing with a major label through independent labels, labels started by non-music entities, or even hiring their own team of music business specialists. Tim seemed to be very positive about OK Go's experience with their label, explaining, "We decided to go the major label route in early 2000, and the one thing we knew then was that we probably wouldn't see much money from the music side of things, but we realized that the majors only come knocking once and they would fund at least one record. We'd be able to get one record and make videos and go on tour. They funded three albums' worth of time for us when we were able to tour the world twelve times over." At the same time, though, he admitted, "I do think that for young independent bands, it behooves them to stay independent and build a following for as long as they can afford to do it, because why give away a piece of what you've got if you don't have to? The more you control creatively and business-wise and financially, I think the better off you are." Tim does acknowledge that there are still some pretty serious roadblocks in the way, stating that "I think the big question right now is how do new bands find funding if they're not going to do a major label deal." Several minutes later, though, Tim did point out that there are answers offered by the Internet: "In this day and age, bands have access to so many free distribution channels. There's even ways to fund projects at places like Kickstarter, where if you've got the desire and a project, you can actually get crowd-sourced funding if you've got a good-enough game plan. That's another way that bands can stay completely independent and make their music pretty much for free and raise money for certain projects that they want to do." Individual projects funded through Kickstarter may not be the same as the kind of backing a major label can give a band while they're touring, but it's a good place to start.

While it may make sense to point bands that are interested in being independent in the direction of OK Go because of their high-profile independence, Tim is careful to note the advantages that they had and also the ways in which they were unique when they started to gain popularity. Reflecting on their career, he told me, "It just so happened that towards our time with the second record that we started making things that we really wanted to make, and because of the Internet we were able to kind of get out of having to ask permission all the time to make things, because all of a sudden there was a place where we could make things and immediately put out online for people to watch, to share. And we did all that while we were still on a major label. So, for a minute there, we were making these homemade videos, and the label was still paying for us to go on tour, and I think that situation was specific to OK Go at the time, and we were able to use it to our advantage, and we were able to build up a following that allowed us to leave the label after our next record. I guess my point is that even though we had the same type of traditional gripes that most bands have with their labels, at the end of the day they didn't do wrong by us for the most part." Having the support of a major label while they started to make a name for themselves through their viral videos is an advantage that most bands aren't ever going to get. While they were able to gain a lot of publicity and fans through their viral efforts, they had the support of a label behind them and the ability to tour without having to personally fund-raise as well as a distribution and publicity system already in place. New bands attempting to build the same kind of Internet buzz will have to do so without those systems in place and won't be able to respond to newfound popularity as quickly or effectively simply because of the lack of resources behind them. Tim points out that one of the big problems with going independent is that if you really do become successful, it can become too much for the band themselves to handle very quickly. "I'm also not naive about the real-life stuff. Not everybody has the kind of funding to keep them going for ages and ages and ages, and the more successful you become, the more in-demand you become and the more it costs to keep yourself out there in the world touring and making records, and you need to find a way to fund that."

How is life on the independent side of the tracks? Some benefits became immediately apparent, as the green-lighting process involved far fewer people. "One of the nicest things about having our own label (which is really just the distribution arm for all our creative ideas) is that we don't have to fight with anyone anymore. Those fights have pretty much gone by the wayside, and we are able to really chase down whatever idea gets us excited in the morning, whether it's photography or a line of shoes or a new record or whatever it is, we don't have to fight about it anymore." Because of OK Go's reputation, there's also a certain level of discussion that's been removed when they do get sponsors for their projects. As Tim explains, "Working with some of these outside sponsors or corporations, most of the time they hire us because they already like what we do and they want us to do what we do. So there's not a whole lot of 'Hey, we've got a creative idea for you guys, what do you think?' It's usually like they come to us and say, 'We want X amount of eyeballs on our business and we know that people love to watch your videos. We'd love to fund something from you guys.'" These arrangements hark back to an earlier time and are mutually beneficial for the band and the sponsor, because, in Tim's words, "the relationship we have with sponsors is sort of a 'patron of the arts' type situation where we make the thing that we want to make and we thank them at the end for making that possible. And we find that usually the businesses, the corporations that we've worked with, are very happy to have that type of relationship with us. Because they know that we get to make the thing that we want to make and we know that they're gonna get several million eye-balls on State Farm or Chevy or whatever." That all said, OK Go does have the freedom to pick and choose who they work with, and this does come into the projects that they get involved with, and Tim knows that might not be the case for all bands. "We're also careful to only get into deals where we know we are going to have that creative freedom. I imagine bands could find themselves in a situation where maybe sponsors do make an effort to curb creative ideas; we're pretty careful to stay out of those situations."

The big question, of course, is if, based on his years of experience, Tim has any words of advice for young groups starting out. And he does! "At the core of it, the very basic and simple idea: make sure you love what you're doing. Well before you get into 'How am I going to fund this project?' do you like what you do? Do you like the people you do it with? If the answer is 'sort of' or 'no,' it's not worth getting into in the first place. Being in a band is probably one of the least likely ways to have a financially rewarding career. If your main concern is financial stability, I'd recommend studying to be a lawyer or a doctor or an accountant. But if music and making things is really what you love to do, then by all means go for it, but make sure you love it, because there's going to be a lot of lean years. It's extremely hard to get people to the point where they do want to fund your project. After that, I would say be as creative as you can, both on the creative side of things and on the business side of things, and be open to alternative methods of funding your project. The day and age of the major label, though they still exist, it's not quite what it used to be. The traditional experience of 'we're going to play clubs until we get the attention of a major label and then they're going to pay for all the things that we want to do'—those days don't quite exist anymore. Being attuned to creative and alternative methods of funding projects is important." I mentioned in the previous chapter his thoughts on sites which, like Indaba, allow users to collaborate on music projects from around the globe, and he also emphasized Kickstarter as a tool for young artists looking to raise funds. "I think it's a pretty awesome idea to be able to have a place to go to raise money to do things that you wanna do and make the things you wanna make. Of the things I've seen recently, that's the one that I think is really beneficial to young bands to raise money for themselves: to make a video or go on tour, or make a record or whatever they're looking to do." But you can't neglect what are now kind of classics. "Obviously there are a lot of, what are now for some of us, old-school methods of getting your name out there. YouTube is still very effective, Facebook is very effective, and Twitter."

One of the biggest tests is still to come for OK Go, as they have yet to record a studio album and release it completely independently. Their previous album (*Of the Blue Colour of the Sky*) was their last album released under contract, and they have released a live album (*180/364*) under their Paracadute label. When I asked Tim if there were plans for a new album, he told me that plans for a new OK Go album were already under way. "We're already writing for it right now, and we begin working in the studio in August, and hopefully we'll have something out in the beginning of 2013." I asked how they were planning to fund this album—through sponsors, fan funding, or other methods—and he admitted, "We're currently working on that… We're looking for alternative ways to fund the whole thing, not only just recording but also touring and video-making as well. We're in the middle of figuring out just how we'll be able to do that." I'm sure there's plenty of fans and music industry insiders who are interested to see how the process goes for them.

OK Go has helped bring a new version of the music business to the forefront, from their skillful use of the Internet to their current method of partnering with non-music companies to help fund their videos, tours, and other projects. Their experiences help show the vast shift the music industry has undergone in the last decade or so, a shift that OK Go got caught in the middle of and managed to come out on the other side with a new way of doing business. Their business model is a one-in-a-million shot, but these days so is getting signed to a label that's willing to invest time and money in you if your first single doesn't take off. Their career also encompasses a few new trends in music business that have emerged in recent years, such as viral videos, corporate sponsorships, and use of social media to build and develop fan bases. Their example isn't one that most bands can follow, but it's a beautiful microcosm of the music business from the years 2002 to 2012.

Chapter 5:

Catch My Disease: Viral Videos

From the beginning of the viral video phenomenon, there has been a music element to many of the videos that have achieved that increasingly common moniker. One of the first viral videos that most people remember was the "Numa Numa" video featuring a young man dancing in a chair in front of his computer to the song "Dragostea Din Tei" by the Moldovan pop group O-Zone. The original video was posted to the site Newgrounds.com on December 6, 2004, and has so far received over 15 million hits on Newgrounds and an additional 48 million on YouTube[17], not counting reposts, versions of the video posted on other websites, or alternate versions. A sample of "Dragostea Din Tei" ended up making it into the mainstream in a bigger way in 2008 in the song "Live Your Life" by T.I. featuring Rihanna. Other popular-music-related viral videos include "Chocolate Rain" and, the infamous "Friday", and countless others that have captured our cultural attention for a few days or even months at a time.

---

17 As of early November, 2012.

Of course, immediate and world-wide distribution has made for its own wrinkle in the music-industry landscape. A perfect example of this was seen 2010 when a young man named Antoine Dobson was interviewed regarding an attempted sexual assault on his sister. The local news segment was put on YouTube, where it gained popularity based on Mr. Dobson's emphatic yet comic threats directed toward the attacker. Then the young men at Auto-Tune the News got hold of the tape, and the hit single of the summer was born. Within weeks, "Bed Intruder Song" was available for purchase on iTunes and was replicated by everyone from individual musicians to marching bands on YouTube. Mr. Dobson and Auto-Tune the News were invited to perform the surprise hit at the BET Awards. By the end of 2010, "Bed Intruder Song" ranked at the top of YouTube's most-watched list, which is even more impressive, because the video didn't come out until August of that year.

This is only one example of the dozens (if not hundreds) of viral videos that have swept across the web like wildfire from Facebook page to tweet to blog post, and everything in between. Some of them are musical in nature, like the above-mentioned "Bed Intruder Song" and the infamous "Friday" as performed by Rebecca Black. Others, like "David after Dentist," fall under different and far more nebulous categories. These videos can have a huge impact on their stars; whether that impact be positive (in the case of OK Go and the considerable amount of exposure they gained through viral videos) or, in sadder cases, negative (the harassment and scorn heaped upon young Rebecca Black seems unnecessary for the crime of singing a poorly written song). How beneficial *are* viral videos? Can a momentary diversion really translate into lasting fame?

Grayson Chance is a musician and songwriter whose career was launched through YouTube. A video of him performing Lady Gaga's "Paparazzi" at a middle-school talent competition lit up YouTube, led viewers to watch videos of his original songs, and ended with his earning a record contract. Grayson was all of thirteen when he co-headlined his first tour with Australian pop star Cody Simpson. His first album was released on August 2, 2011, about two weeks before his fourteenth birthday. Bolstered by high-profile support from people like Lady Gaga and Ellen DeGeneres, Chance's cover of "Paparazzi" has received over 45 million hits. Views of all the videos he's uploaded have topped 76 million views, even though his channel has less than 360,000 subscribers. Perhaps this low number of subscribers compared to video views can help explain the underwhelming performance of Chance's album, *Hold on 'Til the Night*, which peaked at number twenty-nine on the *Billboard* Hot 200. The example of Chance brings up several questions regarding viral video fame and how it translates into album sales and revenue. Are people that willing to pay for what they've become accustomed to getting for free? With the speed that trends move on the Internet, how much time do you have to capitalize on a popular video before the world moves on?

One man who may be in a position to answer that question in the near future is Korean rapper Park Jae-sang, better known as PSY. PSY was a well-established pop star in Korea and on July 15th, 2012 the video for his latest single was uploaded to YouTube. That song was "Gangnam Style" and in the next two months it became clear that something unpredictable was happening. In less than a month the video had gained 25 million views, and PSY was on his way to a meeting with Scooter Braun, the man behind Justin Bieber and School Boy Records. In two months, the video was at 200 million views and PSY appeared on Saturday Night Live. As of early November 2012, the video has more than 600 million views and the single has rocketed up the charts in multiple countries around the world. A song that was a satire of PSY's neighborhood in Seoul, South Korea had resonated with people worldwide. Or, rather, the infectious and silly video featuring PSY performing his "pony dance" had resonated, and the single followed.

PSY was able to capitalize on the popularity of his video not only because he was already an established artist in Korea with a business behind him, but also because he was willing to take meetings, make appearances, and spend the time on the road to promote his single. In the fall of 2012, PSY made appearances at Dodger Stadium, the MTV Video Music Awards, "The Ellen Degeneres" show, NBC's "Today", "Saturday Night Live" and the Australian version of "The X Factor". Whether PSY is able to maintain this level of fame is a question that can only be answered by time, but given how notoriously difficult it can be to break into the American market as a foreign artist his success is noteworthy even with just the one single to his name. It's also noteworthy to see YouTube "break" a single worldwide in this way. It was one of the most popular songs in the country before it was played on any radio station, before it was in any movies, TV shows, or commercials. "Gangnam Style" could be an anomaly, or it could be an example of how music is discovered and popularized from here on out.

When asked about the best way to create a viral video, a YouTube representative said that they've seen that positive videos that make people happy tend to spread faster than ones that are more negative. The popularity and scope of videos featuring adorable animals on YouTube backs up this assertion. For bands looking to make videos, it's also better to keep things positive. Having a negative image or bad publicity might not be a terrible thing once you're a superstar, but if you're just starting out it's best to literally try to make friends. Other tips elsewhere around the Internet include keeping videos short and making a solid stab at humor. It's almost impossible to pinpoint what causes a video to go viral, but if you think about other videos you've seen and felt compelled to share, you can start to understand what people are looking for. Even videos that don't go properly "viral" and become inescapable can make a lot of waves for artists if the videos are interesting and eye-catching. The captivatingly beautiful video for Gotye's "Somebody That I Used To Know" has been shared on Facebook millions of times and is well past 345 million views overall as of November, 2012.

Some people will say that videos that are made for a large audience or that look professional can't be viral, but the gentlemen of OK Go have proven that wrong. Rebecca Black's "Friday" was also clearly a professionally made video that managed to go viral, as was "Gangnam Style". Perhaps viral videos feel more "pure" when they're not intended for mass consumption, but it's not a hard-and-fast rule. While these videos were clearly meant to be seen by a larger audience, the descriptor of "viral" refers to the way the video spreads through the internet, not to the nature of the video itself. And videos can be very successful among a band's fan base even without the kind of viral spread many people are chasing.

Once you get a YouTube account set up, you should aim to become a YouTube Partner. To become a Partner, you have to create original videos that you own all the rights to and that comply with the YouTube guidelines and terms of service, and you have to have a fairly sizable audience. The qualifications say, "You regularly upload videos that are viewed by thousands of YouTube users, or you publish popular or commercially successful videos in other ways." Becoming a Partner, though, gives you access to tools and analytics that aren't available to the average YouTube user and improved revenue streams if you choose to allow advertisements on your videos, so it's useful if you can get there. Growing your audience to the point where you qualify for a YouTube Partner account is very difficult and probably impossible for most groups, so don't be discouraged if it doesn't look like you're going to make it. You can still have ads on your videos even if you're not a Partner, as long as you own the rights to the music in the video (so, only on original songs).

While some independent bands may question whether it's worth the time or energy to record a music video at all, recent studies have shown that having a video available online can be more valuable than previously suspected. In September 2010, a Nielsen survey taken by 26,644 online consumers spread across fifty-three different markets found that 57 percent of people responding had watched an online video in the last three months, and the only other form of digital music consumption that even came close to that number was "downloading a song without paying for it" at 49 percent. This isn't exactly heartening, as it shows that the most popular way for digital consumers to interact with music either entails not paying for music at all or consuming it in a way that could yield a fraction of a cent if the video is watched on the YouTube site itself. But in terms of getting you band out there, it's good to know that people are more likely to play a YouTube video than to stream music (26 percent of survey responders). This doesn't mean that a professionally produced and polished video is a necessity, just that having your music on YouTube through your own YouTube channel with a very basic video will help drive traffic to a source you're in control of and give you access to insight about the users watching your video, how they got there, how long they watched, and so on. If you're writing your own music, it's also a way to earn some very small amounts of royalties, since, as previously mentioned, YouTube pays royalties for video plays on the YouTube website. Embedded clips won't get a payout, and YouTube royalties aren't impressive, but at least you'll be earning something for your music.

As for what kind of videos you should make, the first answer is to record videos for any songs that you feel have broad appeal. Unless you've got a very clear (and easily achievable) concept for a video in mind, don't stress too much about the video itself. There's a ton of videos on YouTube for popular songs that aren't much more than the lyrics over a static image of an album cover or just a static image. If you can get your song up on your website or whatever distribution service you've chosen to use and on YouTube at the same time, do that so that someone else doesn't get the jump on you by putting up their version of your song first. Once you've got some of your own songs on there, a lot of new artists like to do covers of popular songs, because then searching for the song itself will bring up your cover video. I say to do this after you've got some of your own videos up, because if your cover video does catch someone's eye, they can immediately watch some of your videos featuring your own material in that moment that you've caught their attention. You can also make response videos that will show up in the "related videos" bumper for popular videos, so if you're good at making up off-the-cuff ditties about cute cats or people who are still loopy from dental surgery, this could be a good choice.

Non-music options for videos are narrower and probably only interesting to people who are already fans of your music. Behind-the-scenes videos, outtakes of recording sessions, videos of meeting fans at live performances, or anything similar are great if you've got a smallish fan base who are interested in learning more about you, but it's unlikely to attract any new fans. If you are doing live shows, though, you can always encourage your fans to take videos with their phones and put them up online, since then all your fans' friends will see the video through their page.

The problem right now with viral videos is that almost everyone wants to make them, and only a very small group of people succeed; a lot of the time, the people who do weren't exactly trying to. You shouldn't base your business plan around a video becoming viral, but making videos should be part of any independent band's media strategy. This is also an area where there's a lot of possibilities for fan participation and interaction, from asking fans for video concepts, or including fan submitted photos in a video, to encouraging fans to make their own response videos that can help increase the profile of your original video. You never know; one of your local fans may be a budding filmmaker and willing to help you out with videos in exchange for experience and exposure of their own. Even if all you can do is take a photograph and layer your song over it, you've made one more place people can go to hear your music. The one sure thing about viral videos is that videos that aren't made can't become viral, so get out whatever video recording device you've got handy, and get to shooting.

CHAPTER 6:

THE HARD NUMBERS ON FAN FUNDING

At this point, you probably know whether you want to be an artist who releases a single, finely crafted, and obsessed-over album once a decade to a group of fans that barely numbers into the triple digits (if that) or an artist who wants their music to be in near-constant rotation on iPods, computers, and other devices owned by your fans. If you've already put some videos and songs out there for streaming via your various social-media pages and on YouTube, by now you're inching ever closer to the dangerous game of actual distribution. You could self-record and then do a pay-per-unit distribution deal, but you'd like to actually pay the money to get yourself recorded professionally in order to give your fans (and any sponsors you may be looking to approach in the near future) a taste of what you sound like at your best. Professionally recorded and mastered albums don't come cheap, though, so you need a way to raise some funds, and fast—which is how we come to Kickstarter and ArtistShare. Both sites offer artists a way to raise money directly from fans in order to produce an album; in exchange, artists are asked to provide some incentive that's tied to the level of donation received. The sites have slightly different aims and guidelines, so if you're interested in this method of fund-raising, it's best to do some research into both models, which is exactly what this chapter will help you do.

ArtistShare was launched in 2003 with the goal of bringing fans into the creative side of music by allowing them access to the album-making process in exchange for their contributions, which would be used to fund the album. Since 2003 ArtistShare projects by various artists have been awarded four Grammys and nominated eleven times. ArtistShare is also a site that lets artists in by invitation only. Their site features a survey that artists can fill out, which will then be reviewed by a "project management associate" and given a formal evaluation. The benefit of this is that artists who are accepted to ArtistShare can expect a certain level of involvement and guidance from the ArtistShare team when it comes to structuring their project and on ways to more effectively raise funds. Of course, that's if you're accepted to ArtistShare in the first place.

Kickstarter, on the other hand, is available for people with a wide variety of projects rather than just being music-focused. With categories ranging from dance to technology, it's possible to find a niche on Kickstarter for just about any project you may be looking to fund. The site launched in April 2009, and as of January 2012 had over fifteen thousand successfully funded projects. While not as stringent as ArtistShare, the site does have some basic guidelines that all projects must follow, and project proposals are evaluated before they're added to the site to make sure they fall within those guidelines. The broad spectrum of projects on the site may be intimidating to artists, but there is some good news: when the company broke ten thousand successfully funded projects, they released a breakdown of successful campaigns by categories, and music came out on top, with video close behind. The trick behind Kickstarter, though, is that it is based on an all-or-nothing premise. You set a funding goal and a time limit, and you're allowed to exceed your funding goal within that time limit, but if you fail to meet the funding goal in time then you don't get any of the money pledged. In one way this is a good thing: if you absolutely need $3,000 to make an album, it's one thing to not get the money and reevaluate for another attempt; it's entirely another to be obligated to go ahead with the album even if you raise only $1,500. So how have artists who have used the service felt about it?

I talked to Michael Bouchard of the Richmond, Virginia–based band Starfish Prime about their Kickstarter campaign. Rather than using the service to fund an album, they were using it to raise money for a trip to SXSW 2012 to perform in the Sweet Tea Pumpkin Pie showcase. This was the first time the band had used Kickstarter, though they had previously considered doing so, and Michael said that the decision to finally do so came because "we had one month to somehow get $1000 out of nowhere, so I decided if we could get half of that off Kickstarter, we'd be in a much better position. A couple of other bands that are playing with us said they were making Kickstarters, so I figured 'we might as well go for it and see what happens.'" Their original Kickstarter goal was for $500 dollars. When they told their fans about the project, the reaction was positive. While they had only eighteen donors, Michael commented that, overall, "it is a good way to show your support for something, even if you can only donate one dollar. It's the thought that counts, and it was great to see our fans, friends, and family donating. I think it makes the fans feel good, being able to directly help out our cause." Ultimately, the band raised over $1,000, doubling their initial goal of $500 and covering the total cost to get them to Austin for the showcase. They structured the drive with donation amounts from one to fifty dollars and over, and ten of their donors contributed in the over-fifty category, giving them an impressive percentage of contributors in that top bracket.

But are artists who use Kickstarter happy enough with their results to give their assisted fan-funding method another shot? Michael of Starfish

Prime says, "Definitely," explaining, "Now that we already have an account, we just need more ideas! We have been recording our own music for years, but it would be real nice to maybe raise a couple hundred and get a little studio time." As for bands that are considering Kickstarter for their own projects? *"Do it!* I really think it makes everyone involved feel good about what they're doing. Just make sure you keep in mind how much your rewards are going to cost. Also, connect the Kickstarter to Facebook and use other social networking sites to get the link out there. Don't spam up pages, but get the link in as many reasonable places as you can; you never know who might see it and like what you're doing."

The fact that the sites are out there may lead people to believe that it's not difficult to get people to contribute to a fan-funding campaign. Grim experience has proven that for many artists, this is not the case. One artist who worked with ArtistShare had a regular e-mail newsletter that reached somewhere between two thousand and four thousand fans, with similar numbers of fans on Facebook, had only about 150 of those fans actually contribute to their ArtistShare campaign. When asked about the experience of the process itself, sharing material online, finding incentives to share with fans, and following up with fans to try and drum up more donations, the artist said, "The demand of the project was larger than I expected. It was belaboring, because the truth is that, making an album in the midst of working and performing, the last thing on my mind was taking time to document everything and then edit it down to add to the site." When asked about what they thought as far as other artists getting involved with the service, the artist said, "I think it's good for a band if there are five people participating, or for a solo artist who has one or two people helping them on a part-time basis. It was a big demand, without management." The message here is that for a fan-funding campaign, at least for one with the kind of artist-input requirements that ArtistShare has, it's best to have a person who is dedicated to capturing and creating material for the page either on their own or by following up with other members to make sure everything gets done. It's another list of obligations and deadlines to keep in mind, and if a group or individual is actively performing regularly or touring, it can be overwhelming, unless there's at least one person dedicated to that schedule and making sure material gets produced and loaded to the site for fans to watch, read, or otherwise interact with.

There are limits to fan funding, of course. In August 2011, the International Federation of the Phonographic Industry (IFPI) estimated that breaking a new pop act in a major market costs labels around $1 million total. Funding an album for a superstar runs up to $4.65 million. Unless you've got some very wealthy fans or have a million fans you can all talk into sending you one dollar each, matching those numbers is not something the average independent artist can aspire to. But what's a reasonable goal for an ArtistShare or Kickstarter campaign for an independent artist?

Breaking down that $1 million shows that the average recording budget, according to IFPI's numbers, is $200,000. That number is better, but still far out of reach for almost all independent artists. Looking at a breakdown of successful Kickstarter campaigns, there were only twenty-three projects out of ten thousand that raised over $100,000. Over half the successful projects raised somewhere between $1,000 and $5,000, so that range may be the best place to start for an artist who wants to go the Kickstarter route. Goals should be set modestly, since failure to reach a goal will mean you will get no money at all, and the whole process will have been for naught. How much it actually costs to professionally record and mix an album, though, is a difficult question. Recording and mixing costs are usually set by the hour and will vary greatly from studio to studio and can swing wildly even within the same studio, based on what time of day you want to record. Studios will usually also charge more to record a full band (because it's more work for them in terms of setting up all the mics) than an individual or solo performance. There's always the option of purchasing Logic Studio from the Apple store and recording yourself; Logic costs (as of September 2011) $500, and the least expensive Mac that will run it is $600, so that puts you over the $1,000 benchmark right there if you have to purchase both. Never mind that learning how to use Logic Studio properly will take time, and that, unless you've got a band member or close friend who's a recording engineer, it's probably not going to sound as good as it would if you recorded it in a professional studio. If you're just looking to get some music out there for your fans and to build interest in your group until you can launch yourselves more successfully, Logic Studio is a fine solution. If, however, you want a professional recording that you can present to companies in order to get a contract or something that would be high quality enough to secure licensing and synchronization deals, it might be better to put the money toward recording one or two songs you really believe in instead of a whole album.

The ability to record high-quality audio in the comfort of your own home, though, is getting cheaper by the day, so, if you're interested in remaining independent, the investment in equipment is not what it once was and definitely something worth considering. Aside from not having to rely on others for the money to make recordings once you own the equipment, you'll also have the ability to record songs and have them available to the public far more quickly than if you had to go through a studio to get all your recordings made. The other bonus of purchasing and learning to use your own recording equipment is that you can then charge other independent musicians who are not as technologically minded to come record in your home studio—still cheaper than a professional studio and a good way to make back the cost of the investment in recording equipment, besides from selling music. When I was talking to Chris Arbisi of White Trash, he told me that he has been working in a recording studio for years and was still very encouraging of young or new artists working to record their own music. As he put it, "One of the most important parts of the creative process is not to wait to get into the studio; open your laptop and get recording!" Even if you have the resources to get into the studio, it's a great way to get ideas out, so that you can have them available to recreate when you've got your equipment set up, something Chris had experience with, as he told me, "I put the Mac next to the piano, and I put Photo Booth[18] on, and I film myself playing, and I can wait forever to get into the studio, but as long as my idea's captured, that's the most important part of this. Some people wait so long to get into the studio to get everything perfect that the idea is lost."

If you're looking for a way to get into making your own recordings, the tools may be closer than you think. Artist Chris Price recorded his album *Homesick* on his iPhone using an application called 4 Tracks that cost him ten dollars. While discussing it with Buzzbands, Price mentioned the flexibility that recording this way had given him when he pointed out, "The whole world is my studio…. The iPhone gives you a lot of freedom, and it gives you pretty impressive sound quality. It's all about mic placement." Having the iPhone as his primary recording equipment meant that he could record literally anywhere he wanted to, something that is great for making sure you get ideas out when you need to and for playing around with acoustics to make your songs sound the best they can. iPhones aren't just known for their audio-recording quality, either; the cameras on iPhones shoot good-quality video, so creating videos with one is easy as well. Combining a smartphone that has audio and video recording capabilities with a simple mixing app and an external hard drive is a good start as far as recording your own music outside a studio, and raising money to buy those is much cheaper than studio time. Studio recording is always going to give you a richer master with regard to sound quality, but since MP3s or other digital-download formats tend to strip down audio recordings to a lower sound-quality level anyway, you're not losing much if you plan to distribute music online. This technique brings the price point of "recording equipment" down to something that can easily be raised through sites

---

18 A program on Mac that includes both still-camera and video-camera shooting from a built-in camera.

like Kickstarter if you don't already have a laptop, smart phone, or other similar device readily available.

Of course, you can forgo official fund-raising sites altogether and raise funds independently via PayPal or similar means. Going through an official site lends an air of credibility to your project and reassures investors that you're a legitimate project and that there is some oversight and guarantee associated with the money they contribute. That aside, there's not really a downside to putting a PayPal button on your website so that fans contribute if they feel like it or selling your album or other affordable merchandise through your own website. Worst-case scenario: you're no worse than you were before you added the button, and, by putting the button there, you've increased the chance that someone might click on it. This is a less structured way to raise money, as you don't have to offer fans any kind of incentive to contribute, and there's no explicit responsibility on your end to deliver a specific project on a specific date. It's best to stick to selling something, though, even if it's selling stickers for five dollars apiece with the tangential goal of funding an album, because people have gotten in trouble for using a Donate button[19] when they were not an officially approved non-profit organization. Better to save yourself the trouble and sell something inexpensive with a markup and explain to your fans what you're doing, than to risk having your whole PayPal account locked because you violated their terms of service.

One of the things that an artist should look at before pursuing the fan-funding option is how many fans they have information on, and how active those fans are. Social media will be discussed in chapter 8, but looking at how many fans you have on your Facebook, Twitter, or MySpace page can help give you an idea of the support that exists for you if you choose to attempt a campaign. One of the things to remember, though, is that no matter how many fans you have, the chances are that the vast majority

---

19 The Regretsy incident of Christmas 2011 is the best example of this, if you'd like to see one.

of them are not going to contribute a dime to your campaign no matter how many e-mails, messages, status updates, or tweets you send about it. There's a big difference between passive fans and active fans, and an even larger difference between fans who are willing to pay you money and fans who aren't. It sounds callous and unbelievable, but even artists with thousands of fans on their social-media pages or mailing lists can sometimes barely scrape together enough to meet their funding goals when they sign up for one of these campaigns. This is partly because consumers simply aren't used to the business model of being asked to put money up front for an album they'll get later, but part of it is just that there are a lot of people who will click Like or Follow just to be in the loop but who aren't invested in the group or artist.

It's also worth remembering who your fans are before launching a fan-funding campaign; certain demographics are going to have more money to spend than others. If you're looking at a Facebook report that shows the majority of your active users are in the eighteen-to-twenty-four age range, that's not a group that tends to have a ton of disposable income and particularly not at this point in the nation's history. Younger fans or fans well into middle age are more likely to have money that's not tied up paying off student loans or being tossed into that week's ramen fund. For groups with fans in that young adult age range, the low contribution levels offered by Kickstarter may be a more attractive option since fans can donate around five dollars if that's all they can afford. Obviously groups will have to adjust their goal amount with this in mind as well, since one hundred people giving five-dollar donations aren't going to add up to the kind of numbers that one hundred people giving twenty-dollar donations will (or even fifty people giving twenty-dollar donations). Even with these considerations taken into account, timing can play a part. An artist who launched an ArtistShare campaign last year said that in speaking with fans, she discovered "people aren't really that loose with their money these days when it's not a nonprofit," so, before launching a fan-funding campaign, it's best to keep funding goals as conservative as possible and really work to decide what sort of project will be most beneficial. Also, be sure to account for the cost of whatever you're offering for contributions, so you don't get taken by surprise at the end of the campaign when you suddenly have to add in the cost of merchandise. This is easier with Kickstarter, since you won't get any money unless you hit your funding goal, so the cost of fulfilling offers can be rolled into your total budget rather than broken down individually. For ArtistShare it's best to roll the cost of fulfillment into each level, so if one level of donation gets you a CD, T-shirt, and coffee cup, make sure that the donation amount for that level can pay for all of that with enough left over that you're still getting a decent amount out of the donation.

Fan funding is one of those areas where the entrepreneurial nature of independent artists shines through. Sites like ArtistShare and Kickstarter encourage a model that could be seen as venture capitalism writ small. Pitching a project and asking individuals to contribute to it in exchange for merchandise or exclusive access to videos or album release parties isn't exactly seeking investors who will expect their contributions to be returned if the project is successful, but it's pretty close. Really, once you get to the point where you take money from an investor in exchange for a return on their investment, should the project become successful, aren't we right back around to the label model? And when you think about it that way, what's so terrible about labels after all? (More on that later.)

There are always exceptions to every rule: former Dresden Doll Amanda Palmer managed to raise a total of $133,341 to fund a project to profession- ally record a tour she performed with her husband, Neil Gaiman, through a Kickstarter campaign in which she managed to attracted 3,873 backers total. In late spring 2012 she had a campaign that successful crossed the $1 million mark. Her original goal had been $100,000. This time around she had north of twenty-four thousand backers who donated anywhere between one dollar and $10,000. I shouldn't have to spell out for the average reader what advantages Palmer has, but just for kicks, let's mention that both she and her husband enjoy a healthy Internet following. Ms. Palmer is something of a darling on the indie scene and attracts her fair share of attention when she does things like showing up to an Oscars after-party in a sheer dress, as happened on January 17, 2010, and which spread across the Internet like—well, the image of a somewhat famous woman unlucky enough to have her areola exposed on the World Wide Web. As far as exact numbers go, Mr. Gaiman has over 1.7 million followers on Twitter, and Ms. Palmer has well over a half million of her own. Additionally (if we're counting alternate forms of social media despite the fact that there's no good way to track overlap between Facebook and Twitter, given the ease of creating additional e-mail accounts that won't tie back to either), Neil Gaiman has nearly five hundred thousand fans on Facebook, while Ms. Palmer has over a hundred thousand on her own. What does this really mean? Well, mostly it means that Ms. Palmer's success should be taken as the exception rather than the rule; she has an established reputation thanks to her time as a member of the Dresden Dolls, her husband is an international best seller and winner of a slew of literary honors, and between the two of them and their friends they're able to bring a lot more attention to their Kickstarter campaign than most independent artists could ever dream of. Her use of Kickstarter has been something of a slow burn as well, attracting media attention the longer she's at it and the more projects she gets funded. It's encouraging to see the numbers that she's putting up and the eyes that she's attracting to the Kickstarter model, but these kinds of numbers aren't realistic for the average artist.

Fan funding is an incredible tool of the Internet age that gives artists the chance to use their fans as resources in ways that were prohibitively difficult before. The chance to connect with hundreds or thousands of fans across the globe and have them come together to fund an album or other artistic goal is truly inspiring and there have been a lot of words dedicated to the fan funding phenomena that focus on this aspect. What they don't tend to focus on is the increased responsibility the artist bears in terms of delivering incentives to fans who donate, or the fact that most fan funding campaigns have a relatively low participation rate when compared to other measures of popularity available to artists with an online presence. In a lot of ways, the closest spiritual relative to fan-funding campaigns is busking: musicians taking to public areas to perform for the public and leaving a case or bucket open for whatever said public is willing to contribute. As most veteran buskers will tell you, the percentage of the public willing to part with their money to help support you is vastly different than the percentage of the public who hear you and walk by.

CHAPTER 7:

CORPORATE SPONSORSHIPS AND THE CHANGING MEANING OF SELLING OUT

There was once a time when many major bands resisted having their music used commercially, on the basis that they were rebelling against "the system" or "the capitalist overlords," and that if a song of theirs ended up in the latest Coke commercial, it would undermine their message. Their fans would think they had "sold out" and sacrificed their music's integrity on the altar of money. Even as late as the '90s, the idea of a band willingly participating in a corporate sponsorship deal was, in the words of OK Go singer Damian Kulash, "so toxic, that was like the ultimate third rail for a rock band." While big-name partnerships between brands like Pepsi and artists like Michael Jackson may have gotten a lot of press, most artists stayed far away from sponsorships or commercial deals. There are still artists who think that way, but by and large most independent artists I've spoken to have no greater aspiration than getting their song in the hands of someone who can place it in a commercial, TV show, or movie, netting them large payouts in the form of licensing income. So what's changed? How do artists who do rise to fame on the basis of commercial placement feel about this path? Have they been allowed to stay true to their music, or are they expected to change something to make it more palatable for the public? And what are these corporations looking for when they choose to sponsor a band or feature them in advertisements?

One of the more amusing trends in advertising is evident in car commercials that feature songs by bands who were once the epitome of anti-establishment. Whereas being seen as a tool of The Man could sink an artist's career in the '70s, now it's simply what's done. Jimmy Hendrix, Led Zeppelin, Rolling Stones, The Who—all have had their songs used in commercials somewhere around the time their hits moved from the rock stations to the "classic rock" stations. To a certain generation of television viewers, the triumphant scream that kicks off "Won't Get Fooled Again" is most recognizable as the *CSI: Miami* opening theme and won't ever sound right without a quip by David Caruso's Horatio Caine immediately before it. Even the bat-biter himself, Ozzy Osbourne, has come around to not only licensing his music but also has appeared in commercials and brought his family in on the game with a reality series that featured him, his wife Sharon, and their children, Kelly and Jack. Black Sabbath's "Crazy Train" was used in a commercial in which an adorable family on a road trip sang it. Gene Simmons has entered the reality show world as well, but Gene Simmons has always been one on the lookout for a good business opportunity and the KISS brand has, therefore, always been one that was more open to licensing and exploitation.

In addition to licensing opportunities and sponsorship deals, there are also companies who are getting in on the ground floor when it comes to the music industry. Starbucks famously acquired a record label and started their own Hear Music record imprint. While the record sales didn't take off the way Starbucks probably hoped they would, a high-profile record deal with Paul McCartney helped raise the prestige of the label, and everyone who's been to Starbucks in the last several years is familiar with the free download cards at the register or pick-up station and the small rack of CDs carefully positioned next to the cash register for those very lucrative impulse buys. However, the Hear Music label seems to be shifting its focus to working with established artists like McCartney or catalog artists like Ray Charles rather than plucking new artists out of obscurity. The label still boosts a few finds that aren't household names, but Starbucks and Hear Music have probably found that just as people will order the same coffee every time they walk into a store because they already know they enjoy the taste, it's a lot easier to sell them music they already know they like to listen to.

While most are familiar with Starbuck's position in the music world, there are some other companies outside the entertainment world that are getting in on the music game in a big way. Cracker Barrel has a music program that not only signs new artists and distributes their music at all Cracker Barrel locations in the US, but also pursues established artists who may be looking for a new fan base. The company released an album by Smokey Robinson titled *Now and Then* with six songs from his 2009 album *Time Flies When You're Having Fun* and six live recordings of his more classic tunes. While some may dismiss a CD rack in the overstuffed Cracker Barrel stores as not enough to be a serious entry into the music game, Cracker Barrel's distribution has quietly grown to the point where it "has one of the largest footprints in the United States when it comes to physical album sales," according to a December 2010 *Billboard* article. It's not really a big surprise when you consider that the same article also mentions that Cracker Barrel stores average more than sixty-nine hundred customers per store per week and that the CDs are prominently displayed near the cashiers as to make them more appealing to impulse buyers. Part of the reason the program is such a success, though, is careful restriction of the kind of music they're selling. The company's music page lists their genres as country, bluegrass, soul/R&B, and gospel, and there's a total of twenty-one artists listed on their roster, including Dolly Parton and Smokey Robinson—established artists who would require less invest-ment in recording, since Cracker Barrel can simply license existing works or live performances rather than pay for studio time, backing musicians, engineers, and others in order to make an album. Cracker Barrel definitely has an image that they're looking to maintain, and it's unlikely that image will ever expand significantly.

More companies are also working to turn their brand name into a "life-style" rather that just a drink, a car, a clothing line, or what have you, and many are looking to music as a way to begin the process. Toyota-owned car company Scion is launching their own fully functional music company and record label. Scion has worked with musicians since 2003 to produce songs and videos, but they're now looking to add financial support for tours and dealing with marketing and publicity. According to a *Digital Music News* article published on September 28th, 2011, Scion's label will also feature some perks that traditional record labels will be unable to match; they're giving the artists the ability to retain 100 percent ownership of their mate-rial and all creative royalties. They're also planning on distributing record-ings for free, which means that all recording fees and other costs associated with the recordings will be covered by Scion rather than passed along to the consumer. This hands-off approach to music divisions has been seen in record labels launched by Pepsi, Mountain Dew, Converse, and Red Bull as well. The bands are given the support to record, tour, and distribute their music without restrictions or creative requirements placed on their work. For the companies, it's about the buzz they can develop when bands are happy with the business arrangements made and will publicly praise the company without being asked to do so. The advantage for the musical acts is clear; you get all the benefits of traditional label support without as harsh a focus on your record sales, since these companies aren't relying on music as a primary revenue stream.

The model of bands cooperating with corporate entities doesn't have to be as in-depth as a full record deal; there are other ways to use a corporate sponsorship to break into the industry. Getting your song or even your whole band placed in a commercial can be a great way for a struggling artist or group to gain nationwide exposure or at the very least earn a little bit of money. While some advertising agencies may not pay an unknown band much for the use of their material (if anything at all), the group would earn performance royalties anytime their song was heard on television, creating a steady stream of revenue for as long as the commercial ran. Some bands may still hold the view that appearing in commercials shilling a product is a step too far and prefer to stay with a soundtrack only when it comes to their music being used in ads, but there are bands who have decided to take the risk in order to achieve that boost in visibility. Brooklyn-based Matt and Kim had their single "Daylight" featured in a Bacardi commercial and later went on to appear themselves in a commercial for TuneUp that also featured their song "Cameras." Not only did they appear in the commercial with their song, but also they were using the advertised service and extolling its features. Shiny Toy Guns had their cover of "Major Tom (Coming Home)" used in the commercials for the Lincoln MKZ and also recorded a music video that played on the Lincoln website. The Victorious Secrets won a nationwide search in 2010 dedicated to finding a new band for the FreeCreditScore.com commercials. The brand has built a name for itself with catchy commercial jingles that had previously been acted out by actors who didn't sing the songs that became lodged in viewers' minds. Singing about how an up-to-date credit score can improve your life might not be the dream of most musicians, but it does come with a reasonably steady paycheck that one can rely on while writing brilliant songs about anything but credit cards.

Obviously it's not just commercials that can help a band gain exposure; having your song played in a television show has become something of a backdoor to breaking a band. On smaller shows with lower music budgets, the need to find less-expensive options for licensing has driven music supervisors to seek out fledgling bands. Death Cab for Cutie was effectively launched by their high-profile song placements on *The O.C.* and character Seth Cohen's references to the group that peppered the show. The music supervisor for *The O.C.* is a woman named Alexandra Patsavas, and in the past decade she's become a huge tastemaker in the music world without most people ever finding out that somehow all these great songs they keep stumbling across on their favorite TV shows are being found by the same person. Since *The O.C.*, Patsavas has placed music in *Mad Men, Gossip Girl, Grey's Anatomy, Supernatural*, and many other shows. She's also worked on all three Twilight movies. These shows (and the Twilight movies, to a certain extent) have developed a reputation for featuring cutting-edge music from up-and-coming bands that has won them acclaim with fans and non-fans alike. *Grey's Anatomy* in particular likes to call attention to its music selections by the episodes sharing their titles with songs.[20] In spring 2010 they even aired a special musical episode where the characters themselves sang songs that had previously been featured on the show's soundtrack. The special musical episode released its own nine-track album titled *Grey's Anatomy: The Music Event*, which hit number two on the US soundtracks chart with Sara Ramírez's cover of Brandi Carlile's "The Story" entering the *Billboard* Hot 100 at number sixty-nine. The full album also charted on the *Billboard* 200 at number twenty-four with nineteen thousand copies sold. Not record-breaking, but a significant achievement for a soundtrack album that encompassed only one episode of the show and probably a nice boost in publishing royalties for all the original songwriters who had their songs featured on the album. For music featured in televisions shows, you'll receive performance royalties anytime episodes featuring your music are played so shows that go into syndication can be big moneymakers for bands, even if they didn't get a large up-front fee.

To gain more insight into how bands should approach the topic of licensing their music, I spoke to Darren Paltrowitz, who has worked with

---

20 Though the titular song will not necessarily feature in the episode, it's a mark of the importance the writers and producers place on music.

the Hornblower Group, an artist-management company, and asked him some questions about licensing and what new artists would do well to keep in mind if they are approached about a licensing opportunity. When asked about what artists should look for in licensing opportunities, he said "the hope is for the artist to get both a fee for the master use, a fee for the publishing usage, and increased exposure—oftentimes all three are available." This means that the licensor (the individual or group seeking to license your song) would pay the licensee (you) for usage of the master recording and for the right to use the underlying composition, and you would gain increased exposure through the use of your work in their project. Is it worth it to get involved with a project that offers no money up front for master use or publishing rights? "Absolutely; if it's a movie or television show that's going to be run for years, the band will be accumulating a lot of money through ASCAP, BMI, or SESAC. Imagine how much money that would be if you'd been offered zero dollars up front to have your song in *Titanic* or even an episode of *Full House*! Any opportunity where the media—including your recording and/or composition—is going to be prioritized and promoted is a good one."

On the matter of whether artists should be picky about the movie, show, or commercial their music is going to be featured in and if that should enter into their decision to license, Darren offered, "I don't think so. We live in such a segmented world in which market share keeps diminishing. For example, look at how many late-night talk shows there are as of today: Leno, Letterman, Conan, Kimmel, Fallon and Ferguson—and that's without counting what's on paid cable, in reruns in the late night slots, or just in local markets. In turn, what are the odds that someone saw a particular guest? Then furthermore, what are the odds that the viewers are paying enough attention to get the name of what they saw?" Just because your music is used to advertise a particular product or service, or in a show you're not a fan of, doesn't necessarily mean that people will forever associate you with that product or show. Darren went on to say, "Just because a few people yell 'sellout' doesn't mean that a band shouldn't take a pay-check, especially if they are going to take that money and reinvest it into something artistic" such as making their next album, going back on the road, or making a great video. He does advise against trying to tailor your work to what you think advertisers or music supervisors would want, stating that the best way to make your work attractive for licensing is to "be natural. Do what you do very well. If your song is called 'Car Commercial,' I would bet it is far less likely to be used in a car commercial than a song about just generally having a great time, enjoying yourself, or feeling free." Expanding on this, Darren says, "What music supervisors and advertising agencies are seeking is constantly changing, so if you're not hip right now, that doesn't mean you won't be hip in six months.... Some music supervisors want whatever is hot and hip. Other music supervisors want whatever hasn't been discovered and they can claim for themselves. Away from both of these categorizations, someone I know had a song placed in a TV show because the music supervisor had their assistant looking for songs with *California* in the title. Either way, it's a very competitive field."

As far as registering with services that claim to send your music around to music supervisors or others involved in selecting music for projects, Darren discourages it by pointing out that for most music supervisors, "their hope is for the clearance process to be as quick and painless as possible. Multiple rights-holders (e.g., songwriters, record companies, and third party promoters) make it harder. Having a middleman licensing company clearing, [those companies] are most likely working on commission and asking for more money to justify their worth, and that can make it harder." And on the chance that your music is picked up for a commercial, television show, or movie? First of all, review the contract. "'In perpetuity' means forever. Also watch to see if the language is claiming media that hasn't yet been invented." If all goes smoothly, and you agree for your work to be licensed, "review the cue sheets from the music supervisor to make sure the publishing information is listed correctly. Make sure that the song is registered correctly with ASCAP, BMI, and/or SESAC. Take notes every time you see the show, movie, or commercial being aired, and cross-reference that against future PRO statements. Ditto if it's considered a 'union' session, and you're a vocalist or musician that participated in the recording. Double-check all paperwork that comes your way."

While this all sounds complicated and difficult, it can be worth it. Darren described income from publishing rights as "passive income, almost like owning real estate where you don't have to deal with tenants or repairs," because once the composition is linked to media, you'll receive residuals with no extra effort on your part every time the commercial, movie, or television show airs. I also asked him for any parting advice he had for bands that were just starting out, and he offered, "People like working with people that make them feel better about what they do. People like being around people who make them happy. In turn, if you're going to be persistent, remember to be pleasant and to give back when you have the means to do so. Also, remember that some people are late bloomers in the entertainment field—it make take a while to not only make it, but also to discover the voice or the angle that deserves to be heard."

Partnering with corporate entities may once have cheapened an artist's perceived artistic purity, but that's not the case anymore. There's a lot of opportunities out there, and the benefits of "selling out" and having your song featured in a commercial or receiving backing from a non-music company very much outweigh the negatives.

CHAPTER 8:

WHY SOCIAL MEDIA ISN'T MARKETING

So, you've got a Facebook page. Congratulations! So does my grandfather. Social media can be a powerful force that allows you to reach your fans in ways that were previously unheard of, or it can be something that takes up space, time, and mostly just frustrates whoever has to keep updating it with the new version of "Hi! Buy our album please!" that you came up with for that day. When it comes to social media, there's a fine line to walk between promoting yourself and giving your fans things that make them happy, goals which are not necessarily at odds with each other but can be if you go about the promoting yourself part in the wrong way.

The trick you have to remember with social media is this: it is unlikely that you will reach people who *aren't* already familiar with your band, unless you do a good job of catering to people who already *are* familiar with your band. Most people who decided to Like your Facebook page do so because they already know you and want a way to keep up-to-date with what you're doing. These are people you have already reached, and entreating them to

"PLEASE RT!!!!" or "Repost, please!" is, by and large, just going to annoy them. Your fans don't want to feel like you're just using them to get to more people, even if that's exactly what you're trying to do. And one of the biggest things that corporate sponsors are looking for from bands is their social media presence. How many fans do you have? What do your interaction numbers look like? To get into the issue, I'm first going to do an overview of the most popular social networking sites and their basic history. If you are already aware of these (or have watched *The Social Network*) you're welcome to skip the next few paragraphs (or keep a few copies of them handy for those times your older relatives ask you what's that FaceSpace thing everyone keeps talking about).

MySpace was founded in 2003 by a team of eUniverse employees including Brad Greenspan, Chris DeWolfe, Josh Berman, and the infamous Tom Anderson, who became every MySpace user's first friend on the site. An upgrade of the Friendster model, MySpace aimed at a younger crowd and gave users more options when it came to their online space. With the ability to customize profiles with different backgrounds, fonts, and pictures, MySpace quickly gained popularity with young people as a new way to connect and express themselves and just as quickly attracted legions of articles, columns, and op-eds on the kind of generation that would so readily put their lives on the Internet for the approval and edification of others. The site has since seen a sharp decline in popularity as far as social networking goes, as most of its users moved on to Facebook, though MySpace will continue to have a place in the music world for some time. This is because MySpace is also where the independent artist movement began to really gain traction, thanks to the introduction of MySpace Music, which offered performers an easily customizable platform through which they could advertise shows, stream music, link to places to purchase their music, and connect with fans. Instead of having to build a website, you just filled in some boxes, picked a background theme, and you were ready to go. MySpace Music continued to grow over the years, even as Facebook stole most of the casual users away to a place where you didn't have to worry that the friend's page you were about to visit might contain a header gif designed to induce seizures. Even in this very late year of 2012, the music side of MySpace is not only relevant but also growing. After adding a new radio player on December 19, 2011, MySpace announced that they had grown over one million new registered users by February 13, 2012. Of course, that MySpace now allows users to log in using a Facebook account helps as well.

On the heels of MySpace came Facebook, launched in 2004 to college students across the country. Soon afterward came a series of changes that led to the inclusion of high-school students (2005), members of specific companies, and finally membership was opened to anyone over the age of thirteen with an e-mail address on September 26th, 2006. The site continually added new features through these transitions, from the introduction of a news feed soon after the site opened to college populations, to the current version of the site, which includes location tagging, integrated video chat, the time-line profile, and a host of other applications that have all incurred much ranting when introduced but few users actually making good on threats to walk away from it all. One of the changes Facebook made in September 2011 was integrating with Spotify to allow users to share the music they were listening to in a real-time feed on Facebook's news feed. Friends with a Spotify account of their own can simply click the update and begin listening to whatever music their friend is listening to. Through this integration, you don't have to wait for someone to go to your fan page and play music or videos there; with one click they can instantly be listening to your band's music. It's unclear how much of a boost bands can expect from the Spotify integration (if any at all), but there doesn't seem to be a true downside for independent artists to be a part of Spotify and Facebook (at least, beyond the more general Spotify downsides of incredibly low payout rates and potential negative impact on album sales, but that's for chapter 9).

Twitter was launched in March 2006 on the radical idea that perhaps no one wanted to know anything about anyone else that couldn't be conveyed in fewer characters than the average text message. Despite skepticism that the Twitter model could be capable of generating revenue, it was soon crowned a success. As of August 2011, Twitter is actually moving toward an IPO (initial public offering), though they're definitely taking their time about it, particularly after Facebook's underwhelming IPO in the spring 2012. Twitter is plagued by accusations that the company doesn't have any idea what it actually wants to do and serious doubts that the founders of Twitter had a business plan in mind when the site launched. Add to this the fact that around half the accounts on Twitter are basically inactive, and Twitter doesn't seem like a great investment. But it can still be a good tool for a band looking to find new ways to connect with fans, especially if you can utilize the hash-tag system effectively so that people doing locations or topic searches can easily find your relevant tweets.

In July 2011, Google launched their second attempt at a social network (they would prefer we ignore the short-lived Google Buzz) called Google+. Taking the "build a profile about yourself" approach from Facebook and the "random people can follow you and you can't do anything about it" approach from Twitter, Google+ began on an invitation-only basis. This, of course, caused nearly everyone on the Internet to demand an invitation and, ironically, take to Facebook to complain and/or gloat about whether or not they had made it onto Google+. Since then, Google+ has worked to offer services that can't be found on other social media sites, like video hangouts with up to ten people complete with integrated YouTube (so you can all watch the same video together) and Google Documents. Right now Google+ doesn't offer any integrated music apps, which puts its technology behind Facebook's. They definitely have the opportunity for integration with the Google Play music store and music player, since those are both connected to Google accounts and could be further integrated into Google+. At the time of this writing, though, that's not the case.

LinkedIn is a little different in that it's a "social" media site that's actually not meant for socializing but for business-related networking. Bands that are gaining success and attention may want to use LinkedIn as a way to connect with possible corporate sponsors or even industry insiders. Posting on LinkedIn your albums, live shows, reviews, and so on is a great way to consolidate all that information for people you'd like to work with in a business capacity—and if any of your fans happen to be in the industry, it's an easy way to make your business information accessible to them. Moreover, it's a good way to convey the message that you're serious about the business side of your music. Joining groups focused on the music industry can also be a good way to find out a little more from people who are already successful.

While toiling away creating profiles and updates for social media may seem like the opposite of what a new artist wants to do, neglecting these resources out of fear or out of a sense that you're "above" Twitter or anything else can hurt your career. Like it or not, there is an expectation that groups have a profile on Facebook and a Twitter stream that fans can use to keep up with their shows or new material. It's a sad fact that the ability to promote yourself extensively online has now shifted to an obligation to do so, lest fans or other observers come to the conclusion that you're not "serious" about getting yourself out there.

A common refrain you'll hear when it comes to social media is how you can use it to "monetize" your fans. (You won't hear that from me, because I hate the word *monetize* and everything it stands for.) For new artists, the thing to focus on with social media isn't how it can make them money, since it most likely won't, but how it passively collects information on your fans and what they want to see or hear from you. Most of the important statistics on your page are already tracked by whatever your preferred social-media site happens to be (unless it happens to be Twitter), so all you have to do is find the place on your fan page that says "analytics" or "stats" or something similar. Facebook uses the term *insights* because they enjoy being different and confusing. These breakdowns will include information on how your fans break down by age, gender, and usually general location. There will also (for Facebook) be information on what percentage of fans interacted with your posts in some way versus how many actually saw them and how they came to see the post. These statistics can help you determine what your fans are interested in on your page and what information is more likely to spread over that outlet.

While Twitter doesn't have a good way to see how people are interacting with your tweets beyond whether it was retweeted or if someone directly replies to you, there are some third-party services that will connect to Twitter for you and provide that information. One of the more popular is Hootsuite, which you can also use to connect to Facebook, LinkedIn, and other social-media sites, so that you can write an update once and have it spread across all those sites at the same time. Whether this is strictly advisable or not is a matter of opinion, since the sites work in slightly different ways so it can be worth the extra time to customize updates to each site. Hootsuite also provides some basic analytics with their free account, including how many people clicked on any links you embed through the Hootsuite template, and where those clicks came from. Their premium account offers more in-depth information and the ability to create simple-to-use reports showcasing statistics for your social-media interactions. Tweetdeck is another popular Twitter tool that offers many of the same abilities, and both Hootsuite and Tweetdeck have tie-in apps for smartphones so you can update on the go.

In addition to these standard social-media platforms, there are sites like Tumblr and Pinterest that have emerged. Tumblr is described as a "micro-blogging" site where people can not only create their own content but re-blog the content others create on their own pages. Pinterest is similar; users create "boards" that they can "pin" things they like to and organize their boards by topic—a sort of virtual scrapbook. Because of the differences, Pinterest and Tumblr not going to be used the same way sites like

Facebook and Twitter are; many bands have their Facebook and Twitter accounts set to send messages out anytime they update their website, and that's not exactly going to work for sites like Tumblr or Pinterest. Tumblr seems best for sharing short bursts of information, such as show dates, that can then be re-blogged easily without losing context or information. Images and video also work well on Tumblr, so it's a nice way to document making an album or the experience of being on tour if you find that you've got a fan base that includes a lot of Tumblr users. Otherwise, those things can (obviously) still be shared on Facebook. Tumblr also features a great deal of fan-created art or media, so even if you don't put your own material on Tumblr, it may end up there anyway. As long as it's still attributed to you, that's not a bad thing. Pinterest can give you a way to share with fans things that inspire the band members, your favorite places to hang out, or just other groups that you enjoy so they can get a more personal view of the band and what goes on behind the scenes. It can also let fans pin your material to their boards and give you a chance to see a little more about what your fans are into. There are some pretty broad stereotypes about both services regarding who they're attracting. Tumblr tends to be teenagers and geeks, and Pinterest is very popular with women, particularly women planning weddings. It's up to your band to decide if it's worthwhile or not to pursue these sites in addition to other social media, and if there's a way for you to figure out in advance if your fans use them, it'd be good to do so. The more social media you're trying to keep up with, the more work there is, and it can end up causing a lot of stress for not a lot of payoff in terms of increased popularity. If you've got a lot of fans using these sites, that means you've got a lot of people likely to disseminate what you post on them, which can help increase your fan base, but that's a big *if*.

The simple explanation for how to use social media is to use it to give fans what they want. Do your fans want information on your shows? Pictures of you and your band-mates goofing off in someone's backyard? Videos of acoustic, impromptu performances showcasing a stripped-down version of your song? A site that features fan-made videos or photos of people at concerts that they can tag themselves in? It's a question all bands or artists will have to figure out on their own. It usually isn't even as simple as asking fans what they want from your social-media page or website, since many fans aren't even aware of what they want in the first place. Analytics can help you see what fans are clicking on or commenting on more frequently, which is a good start, and for a while you may have to adapt the "throw everything out there and see what sticks" philosophy in order to figure out exactly what people are looking for.

As many bands have already discovered, though, a large number of Facebook fans or YouTube views don't necessarily translate into album sales. While someone might be happy to click Like on your post or watch a video you tweet, when it comes to putting up actual money, there's plenty of folks who won't bother. There's not much you can do to persuade them. Since most serious fans will be willing to spend what they can on your music or shows (see chapter 14, on being a better fan, for more tips), it is best to keep mentioning if you have a single available for sale somewhere or ask fans to help support your fan-funding campaign if you choose to start one, but don't assume that having five thousand fans on Facebook means that five thousand people will be donating to your fan-funding campaign or even buying your album, once it's completed. One thing that could help streamline this process is a plug-in for Facebook pages called "Impulse," by a company named Moontoast. This plug-in feature allows artists to sell their products through a storefront directly within Facebook and design custom offers that make the best use of the medium[21]. For bands that have products to sell and active Facebook pages, this is definitely worth looking into, given the popularity of Facebook. According to comScore, Facebook had 163 million unique US visitors in September 2011. Twitter lagged behind with 32.3 million, and the somewhat enigmatic and self-perpetuating Tumblr put up 14.3 million. Marketing directly through Facebook

---

21 More information can be found at http://www.fanimpulse.com/.

makes a lot of sense, given how much time people spend on the website and how much money people have already dumped into Facebook games such as Farmville. There's a lot of potential there, and capturing sales where people more naturally look for your information is a clear benefit for any artist's business plan.

One of the common downfalls of social media is that having a way to instantly communicate any and all thoughts to the world is not a good thing for everyone. There have been many stories of minor public-relations disasters when a star took to Twitter with an ill-advised joke or insult. Avoiding these situations is mostly common sense; always remember to never post angry, and that everything you put on the Internet will not die. Even if you delete the post or tweet, there's no surefire way to undo the damage that can happen, and you can never guarantee that someone didn't grab a screenshot for the purpose of preserving your misstep for posterity. A good way to work around this is to plan out tweets or posts in advance and then use a site like Hootsuite or Tweetdeck to schedule them, so you're not actively posting throughout the day and less likely to give in to a sudden impulse to tear someone a new one. Don't respond to trolls, but pay attention to people who may have a legitimate complaint or question that's just phrased poorly. Finally, by and large it's best to steer clear of politics, because there's no way you won't make someone angry. Some bands have made a habit of deliberately pissing people off and feeding off the outrage for publicity, but that works better if you've got a devoted fan base that will rally around you.

People inside and outside the music industry are paying attention to Facebook numbers. As Dan Rose, the vice president of partnerships at Facebook, said at Midem, "I think there's a new currency that's emerging in the music industry, which is how many people have shared a given song or a given artist on Facebook.... The currency is going to become the new way that people talk [about] whether the music [is] blowing up, and we're just at the beginning of that now." He went on to say that there had been about five billion songs shared through Facebook in the last four months and imagined how that would keep growing over the months and years. Looking at the top ten songs shared on Facebook in 2011, Skrillex had two entries on the list, according to the *New York Times*. While the vice president of partnerships at Facebook has a pretty hefty incentive to push Facebook as part of the new music industry currency, the sheer volume of numbers involved would indicate that it is worth artists' time to get their songs out there for people to share. And when polled by *ReverbNation* and *Digital Music News*, a collection of over two thousand randomly sampled artists rated Facebook connects as more valuable than other forms of connections with fans, including YouTube, Twitter, mailing lists, MySpace, and Google+. There's no data on how or why the artists made that decision, though—whether they felt their fans were genuinely more engaged on Facebook or whether they were just more comfortable with the platform.

The biggest thing to remember with social media is that it's there to help you make yourself available to your fans wherever your fans are. Once you get a Facebook or Twitter account, it's not a terrible idea to post a little "so where do you hang out online?" post to see how involved your fans are. For bands targeting younger demographics, things like Tumblr may be something worth looking into, but if your fans are older then the site probably isn't one they're going to be using on a regular basis. If a Tumblr is never re-tumbled, does it really matter? The short answer is no; the longer answer is that it really depends on what your goal is, and if your goal is to gain exposure (which is should be), then stretching yourself thin over every social media or social-media-related site out there isn't going to help your band if your fans aren't using it. Additionally, attempting to master every form of social media out there on your own is a good way to drive yourself crazy. Devising a cohesive and achievable social-media strategy that covers only one or two sites is preferable to throwing up profiles, pages, or blogs with no plans on how to follow through or how they're going to be updated or developed as your career moves forward.

Social media offers some incredible opportunities for bands and fans that would have been impossible only a decade ago. Building relationships with a fan base has never been easier, and bands are rightly taking advantage of all the tools at their disposal. Like any other business endeavor, social media is best when approached with a clear plan and strong attention to detail.

CHAPTER 9:

THE NEW RADIO: SATELLITE, INTERNET, AND EXTRA-TERRESTRIAL

While many independent artists don't come up with a strategy for radio, assuming that in this day and age it's an obsolete medium, it's foolhardy to suggest that there's nothing to be gained from it at all. It's not a coincidence that the most frequently played songs are also almost always the top-selling songs on online distributors like iTunes and Amazon. (I will admit that the cause and effect there is a bit murky, but it's not a coincidence in either case.) More to the point, while terrestrial radio stations have undergone a massive amount of consolidation in the last decade or so, there has also been an increase in several forms of alternative radio that offer opportunities that independent artists should not ignore. Sirius, Pandora, and even the new terrestrial channels that filter between bandwidths on HD radios are all outlets that should be considered. And while they are thin on the ground, independent radio stations should be targeted in an effort to build a relationship that can lead not only to airplay but also to local shows and promotion on their website that will benefit the band or artist. In short, radio is not dead; it's just undergone a bit of a makeover.

Of course, what has been meant by the term *radio* has changed over time. The very first radio station was started in Britain on the Isle of Wight in 1896 by Guglielmo Marconi. At this time, I am 99 percent certain that everyone reading this book grew up with radio. The first US commercial radio broadcasts began in the 1920s, and radio's popularity grew rapidly for the next several decades. In the original sense of the word, *radio* refers specifically to the transmission of signals through space via the modulation of electromagnetic waves, which possess frequencies below the threshold of visibility. Once radio receivers became common in the US, the term *radio* was used to refer to the physical radio receivers themselves. Eventually, *radio* referred to both the medium and the physical receiver—which is somehow less confusing than it sounds. Now, of course, radio simply refers to a style of music delivery that is not on-demand or listener-created and is broadcast from a centralized source to listeners in disparate locations, whether that broadcast is in traditional electromagnetic wave form and divided up into AM or FM options (via a satellite that can reach receivers spread out across the continent, if not the world) or through the Internet, where people can access the signal globally as long as they have an Internet connection with a reasonable amount of bandwidth. Some of these services are free, some are paid for, but all of them have fallen under the heading of "radio" in modern times, and they're all worth independent artists' consideration, if only for the performance royalties that radio-play generates. That is, if you write your own music. If you're only playing covers, then you might want to skip this chapter.

One of the advantages that traditional FM radio had over Internet and satellite radio was that every car in America came installed with an AM/FM radio. To listen to Internet radio in the car, you need a smartphone of some kind with an app that plugs into your car's sound system, and with satellite radio, consumers previously had to invest in a new receiver that replaced the old radio for their car. However, thanks to deals with a laundry list of automakers running the gamut from Kia to Bentley, Sirius radios are coming either preinstalled or as part of an options package in 65 percent of new cars sold in America. Most of these cars will come with a complementary subscription for a time, and then give the auto owner the option to pay for further service. As of August 2011, Sirius announced that in the face of the recession and Americans' cutting back on most forms of discretionary spending, they expected to add 1.6 million subscribers by the end of the year. At the time of the announcement, the company boasted over 21 million subscribers already. Sirius does offer many advantages over traditional radio for listeners; while they have 239 stations, all of those 239 stations remain the same no matter where you go. You don't have to worry about driving out of range while a song you love is playing or fiddling with the Seek button to find something to listen to. Sirius also has their music stations broken down by genre pretty rigidly, so there's no danger that, for instance, in your travels you'll end up somewhere that features only country stations or only Spanish-language stations.

Sirius's numbers seem like small potatoes compared to the 100 million registered users boasted by Pandora; however, nearly all of Sirius's subscribers are paying, with a smaller percentage still in the free-trial stage. While Pandora does have paid options, they have not released hard numbers on how many users are paying thirty-six dollars a year to have access to the ad-free unlimited Pandora One service. Every Sirius subscriber is paying a minimum of $12.95 a month for their service, which comes out to $155.40 a year. That means that, if there are 21 million paying subscribers, Sirius is clearing somewhere around $3 billion a year on subscription fees alone. To earn at the same level, Pandora would have to sign up around 90 million Pandora One subscribers.

Of course, for the independent artist, it's not about the numbers the stations are putting up, it's about the number of ears listening, and in that regard Pandora is clearly winning. Both services feature information on how artists can submit recordings on their websites, with Pandora's specifications being far more stringent than Sirius's due to Pandora's "buy now" feature with the songs they play. The big question, though, is how much of a chance does a submission stand of being accepted? Unfortunately, that's not a question that can be answered at this time. Pandora does not publicize information about how many submissions they accept versus how many they receive, although I was able to find out that 95 percent of the tracks that Pandora has on file play on a monthly basis. So the good news is that, if you do manage to get your music accepted by Pandora, there's a 95-percent chance that someone will hear it at least once a month.

Spotify, a popular music subscription service that originated in Europe, also recently made their entrance in the US with a staggered, invitation-only approach similar to the one adopted by Google+. Spotify offers a basic service that allows users to listen to music on their desktop while connected to the Internet for free, but features advertisements between songs and on the player itself to support the licensing fees. Spotify also offers paid subscriptions at two levels: the "Unlimited" account that allows you to listen to an unlimited amount of music without ads for $4.99 per month, and a "Premium" account for $9.99 a month that boosts better sound quality, unlimited plays, a mobile app, offline mode, and the ability to export your playlists to other devices. This model, with different levels of features available at different price points, is a smart way to target the broadest range of consumers who are interested in a subscription music service. For artists looking to get their music on Spotify, the company has a list on their site of music aggregators that provide music for Spotify, such as TuneCore and CDBaby, along with several others mentioned in chapter 3.

Spotify has gotten some negative press in the music world over what some allege is preferential treatment for major labels over independent labels, and some independent labels even went so far as to pull all their music from the service. While I can't speak to the veracity of the allegations (though I will say that I wouldn't be surprised in the least if they were true) it is a question that independent artists may want to ask. What, if any, is the benefit of making my music available on Spotify? Yes, they do pay artists when their songs are streamed, but, realistically speaking, what kind of money are we talking about? Not much, is the short answer. The breakdown on what artists are paid for their songs is in the fractions of a cent per stream, which means that unless you've got a high volume of listeners, you're not going to see any significant income from Spotify, so it's best to not look at the service as a source of income. There's even been some discussion that availability on Spotify could lead to people not purchasing albums, but that's something that each band will have to figure out for themselves and discuss with their fans. Frankly, I happen to think that if people can't find the music they want to stream for free online, they're more likely to pirate it than buy it, but that does depend on the consumer.

In an attempt to get in on the radio-on-demand trend, Clear Channel launched the iHeartRadio app, which they heavily promoted across all their radio stations plus a massive concert in Las Vegas held on September 23 and 24, 2011. With radio-friendly headliners like Lady Gaga, Jay-Z, Coldplay, The Black Eyed Peas, and Nicki Minaj, and with radio stations across the country giving away ticket packages that could also be won by joining the app's Facebook fan page, the amount of money that's been poured into promoting iHeartRadio was staggering. Promising the ability to listen to any radio station connected to their network in the US from anywhere and a future ability to build playlists, iHeartRadio is emulating not only Pandora and Spotify but also SiriusXM, which has long held the advantage that you can listen to the same Sirius station across the entire country, as mentioned previously. With iHeartRadio, if the promises are to be believed, you'll be able to do the same with your favorite FM station as long as your favorite FM station is one of the 750 stations that are included in the app. With players designed to work on your computer, iPhone, iPad, Blackberry, Android phone, Windows phone, and some wireless-enabled sound systems, the iHeartRadio app is not groundbreaking in the true sense of the word, since almost all these devices already have radio apps available for them. Since the app will be streaming radio stations from across the country and since the company's site doesn't mention anything to the contrary, it appears that the downside to this will be that you'll be experiencing the typical FM-radio level of commercials. Both Spotify and Pandora have commercials in their free versions, but they're generally few and far between, whereas anyone who has spent time listening to FM radio knows that it's up for debate whether the stations play more ads than they do music at certain times of the day. Right now the app is completely free across all platforms, so it's safe to assume that most of the revenue will be coming from advertising.

There is a way that the iHeartRadio app will be beneficial to artists and labels who are struggling with cash flow; while terrestrial radio is not required to pay for performance licenses for the use of the master recording, digital radio is. This means that when your song gets played on Pandora, there's a small amount of money that will be earned both by the songwriter for use of the composition and by the artist themselves or the owner of the master recording (if it's a different person) for use of the master recording. FM radio has not had to pay a master use license, since the music industry saw radio as a promotional tool for so long and did everything they could to encourage stations to play their music early and often. Not only did they not enforce a performance license on master recordings, there was rampant bribery taking place, where the labels were paying radio stations to play songs. This was a huge scandal that achieved a lot of public attention in the mid-twentieth century. Of course, like many things in the music industry, the legacy of payola was far longer than most people realize.

Technically, it is still legal for a song to be played in exchange for monetary compensation, but the compensation must be disclosed on air as sponsored airtime, and the song cannot be considered part of regular airplay under US law 47 U.S.C §317. Surprisingly enough, most record labels found ways around this law, most frequently by offering non-monetary compensation to radio stations in the form of tickets or other merchandise that the station could use for give-aways, or by employing third-party independent record promoters. These third-party promoters would generally exchange money with radio stations in order to promote their client's music, but since the money didn't come directly from the record labels themselves, it didn't technically violate the law. The labels exploited this loophole, and radio stations benefitted greatly from these "promotional efforts" for far longer than most people realize. In 2005 former New York State Attorney General Elliot Spitzer began targeting payola violations in his district. In 2007 the FCC investigated the issue and established that the use of independent radio promoters was still a violation of the law. Fines were levied on four radio companies (CBS Radio, Citadel, Clear Channel, and Entercom) in the amount of $21.5 million dollars, and tougher restrictions were put in place for those fined companies, none of which actually admitted any wrongdoing.

While traditional radio still doesn't owe performance royalties to recording artists for playing songs, digital radio does require performance royalties to be paid, so any radio broadcasts that are streamed through the Internet or via the iHeartRadio app are going to fall under that heading. The organization in charge of collecting these royalties (as well as royalties from satellite radio and the music channels of digital cable or satellite TV) is SoundExchange. Anyone performing on a recording, whether they wrote it or not, and entities or individuals who own the copyrights to their sound recordings should be sure to register their work with SoundExchange to make sure that they receive any royalties that may be due to them. There are some companies that pay digital royalties directly rather than going through SoundExchange, but registering with SoundExchange along with a PRO means that you've got all your bases covered with regard to digital performance royalties.

As mentioned in chapter 8, MySpace Music has also gotten in on the Internet radio trend. They launched a radio player for their site on December 19, 2011, and then announced that they had seen a large jump in registered users since that date. MySpace already has a large amount of name recognition when it comes to music, though, and even with that recognition, they've integrated a Facebook app to allow users to register using a Facebook account rather than creating a separate MySpace account.

What's going to matter more for all these various forms of "new" radio is whether or not people are actually interested in listening to them. Streaming music online still accounts for a fairly low percentage of all digital music consumption, in the September 2010 Nielsen survey referenced in chapter 5, only 26 percent of survey takers said they had listened to streaming music online in the last three months. That's a pretty wide window of time, so the fact that barely over a quarter of responders could say that they'd listened to streaming music in that time is somewhat disheartening. In the last year, there have been new services offered in the US (such as Spotify) and advancements in technology with smartphones and other Internet-connected portable devices that may begin to turn that number around. While people might not listen to streaming music on their desktop frequently, if they can plug their phone in and stream Pandora or Spotify through their car's sound system, they could be more likely to take advantage of the service.

It's clear that Internet radio is growing, and, as with anything new, there are some growing pains. Debates are still raging over whether Spotify is ripping off artists or having a negative impact on record sales, and the more streaming services that emerge, the more the argument is going to be spread around. The problem of payout with streaming services is mostly a problem with short-term versus long-term earnings; someone buying your single through iTunes will result in a lump payout of somewhere between seventy cents and a dollar. Once the single is bought, though, the person can listen to that song in perpetuity without ever paying for it again as has always been the case with purchasing recordings. When you listen to Spotify, every time the song is played, it earns another fraction of a cent. The number of plays that you have to have on Spotify to reach the same amount of profit earned from the purchase of an iTunes single is around 275 streams. To equal the money earned from an iTunes album purchase, your single would have to be streamed somewhere in the neighborhood of 1,845 times.[22] And those earnings are likely to be spread out over time rather than paid out in a lump sum the way digital purchases are. There's also the feeling that making music available on Spotify or through other streaming services will cut into record sales, but most of the evidence is anecdotal. On one hand, you can say that Coldplay held their album *Mylo Xyloto* off streaming services for a certain period of time and saw huge sales numbers. The same goes for Adele, whose album *21* has had record-breaking sales numbers and is not available on Spotify as of February 2012. At the same time, Lana Del Rey's album *Born to Die* was available for streaming before it was released, and still saw sales numbers that pushed it to the number two position on the *Billboard* charts when it was released. It's a debate that won't end anytime soon, and an issue that all bands or artists must decide on for themselves if they're going to be independent.

One of the things that might tip artists in favor of Spotify is how hard the service is working to promote itself around the world. In the first quarter of 2012, they announced a lot of new developments and a high profile partnership with Coca-Cola. Part of the agreement includes that "Coca-Cola has committed to promote Spotify in paid media and through its massive distribution network," so this could be a much bigger win for Spotify than for Coca-Cola. The benefit for Coca-Cola appears to be the "cool" factor of being associated with Spotify, as the report of the deal published in AdAge on April 18th, 2012 mentioned that "Spotify will be the centerpiece of Coca-Cola's 'Year of Music' campaign in 2013.... Music has been central to Coca-Cola's efforts to reach teens, a demographic group projected to

---

22 According to *Billboard* article "The Bottom Line" in the February 11, 2012 edition.

represent one-third of the global population by 2020." This means a lot of kids being reached by an ad campaign targeted directly at them, and a lot of kids being exposed more explicitly to Spotify in particular. It's unlikely the company would ever be able to achieve this level of publicity on their own. Spotify has been working hard to develop partnerships with global brands. In addition to their integration with Facebook (which promises to become deeper with a set of new features such as a Play button for artist pages that would lead directly to Spotify or one of the other integrated streaming services), they've also been working to develop Spotify-based apps for companies such as AT&T, McDonald's, and Intel. With the low rate of premium subscribers, some had been wondering how Spotify would become successful, and this flurry of partnerships and agreements gives us a pretty clear answer. Daniel Ek, the founder and CEO of Spotify, is clear about what the goal of these arrangements are: "To bring people free music while being sustainable so artists can make a living, someone has to pay for it." For those who doubted that Spotify would be able to make the jump from niche distraction to mainstream music service, it seems they're doing everything to prove them wrong.

While Spotify has gotten a great deal of press lately, both positive and negative, it's hardly the first player in the streaming game. In the US, Rhapsody is still the confirmed largest streaming music service,[23] with over a million subscribers and ten years of history behind it. Using a ten-dollars-a-month access model similar to Netflix, they offer connection with any Internet-enabled device and apps for all major categories of smartphones. Rhapsody was also one of the very first streaming services launched way back in 2001, and suffered some initial poor publicity due to the lack of material available on their service and other streaming services—at least in comparison to Napster, which was still available at the time. Since then the service has grown and offers both the monthly streaming service and sales

---

23 Spotify has more users worldwide, but hasn't provided a breakdown of how many of them are US based.

of individual MP3s. However, with new options springing up regularly, it's questionable how long Rhapsody will manage to hang on to a piece of the subscription music market.

One of the more interesting innovations in streaming music has come from a surprising source; the cell phone carrier Cricket has developed Muve Music, a service that offers unlimited music downloads to your phone, as well as the ability to share playlists with other users, create your own ringtones and ringback tones from songs you've downloaded, and have access to new music sent directly to your phone. The cost of the service is built into the phone plan, so you don't pay individually for anything you download. Muve already has over half a million subscribers, making it the second-largest music subscription service in the US (behind Rhapsody), and Muve is looking to expand internationally. The bundled model, where the streaming service is included in the monthly cost of the phone plan rather than allowing users to download songs or albums a la carte, is a model that could work for other phone companies and music subscription services. iPods had a huge advantage over CDs due to the much higher storage capacity, but why bother with the storage capacity if you can access any song you want anywhere with your phone? Additionally, Muve's service gives consumers the ability to download songs and create playlists without a computer to synch with. For people whose phones are their primary means of connecting to the Internet, this is big news. Right now Muve is working exclusively through record labels, both majors and independents, but perhaps, in the near future, we'll see services like Spotify and Rhapsody that already have clear inroads for independent artists partnering with cell phone companies to offer similar services.

The bottom line on radio for independent artists is that Internet and digital-radio services are more accessible than traditional FM radio in terms of getting your music to them, even if you have no guarantee it will be played. Unfortunately, as reported by a joint study by NPD Group and NARM released in November 2011, most music discovery is still happening on FM and AM radio stations, even among music fans who are considered the most "committed" and who spend a significant amount of money on music and live shows every year. Over 50 percent of users who met those conditions said that traditional AM/FM radio was influential in their music discovery process. The next two items on the list were friends, family, and/or coworkers who played songs for them (just under 50 percent) with YouTube, Vevo, and other online video sites trailing at just under 40 percent. Spotify and iTunes were not on the list, but for Spotify that may be due to when the survey was conducted. For older users, the percentage influenced by radio jumped to nearly 75 percent, with friends, family, and coworkers a distant second at just over 40 percent. No websites even cracked the top ten on that survey, with the other spots filled out with movies, TV shows, satellite radio, and music heard in public places. There's a point to be made here about the nature of music and technology news and the fact that no one likes to report on things that are perceived as boring. "Many people still listening to FM radio" doesn't grab readers and get clicks like new numbers of Spotify subscribers or updates on Pandora's mobile app. Just looking at the numbers for various streaming services should make that clear; combine the 2.5 million worldwide Spotify subscribers, the one million Rhapsody subscribers, and the half million MUVE subscribers, and you still have substantially fewer subscribers to these digital digital-streaming services than people who have listened to the radio in the last month or who have watched the latest Justin Bieber video on YouTube. Those of us in the industry all want to be perceived as cutting-edge and on the next page before everyone else, and occasionally we can be so focused on looking ahead that we don't take the time to look around and see that the people we're trying to reach aren't there with us. It's worth the time to seek out local radio stations in the area that play music similar to yours (sending your music to the local NPR station when you're a thrash metal band isn't necessarily wise) not only for the inconvenient fact of the continued strength of radio on influencing music fans, but also because these stations usually coproduce or sponsor concerts and festivals in the area. The Internet has opened up a whole new way for artists to reach fans and spread their music, but getting too deep into the digital world can mean neglecting potentially important relationships in the physical realm, and the smart independent artist should make sure not to make that mistake.

CHAPTER 10:

WHY LABELS WON'T DIE, AND WHY THAT'S A GOOD THING

Most artists know, if they've attempted to make it on their own, that raising the money for an album or tour is really only step one. Once you have the money, you still need to pay for a tour coordinator, a publicist, a manager, musicians, music engineers, venue and/ or studio fees, an ad agency, and more in order to have something close to successful come out of your effort and money. Independent artists have to find these people on their own, take their own meetings, and do a significant amount of planning on the project themselves. This leaves less time for them to be artists—to do that thing that they do best. And once all this is said and done, the artist still has to do all the accounting, unless an affordable accountant, familiar with the music industry, can be hired, and that's obviously another expense that needs to be budgeted for.

Labels eliminated all these problems. Of course, the trade-off in terms of artistic freedom and reduced percentage of revenue from one's product is not to be underestimated. When self-distribution was functionally impossible to achieve, labels were able to leverage their abilities to a position of great power over their roster of artists. Now that the Internet has by and large eliminated the problem of distribution for independent artists, labels find themselves scrambling to recover from the blow to their income and their draw for artists. Obviously, previous business models have been based primarily on the income from record sales, which made labels incredibly weak financially, something many of them realized only in retrospect. However, we can now see the real value of labels in terms of their abilities other than distribution.

As mentioned in chapter 6, one of the biggest things labels can bring to the table is cold, hard cash. A label breaking a new pop act typically spends around a million dollars between recording costs, tour support, promotion, marketing, video production, and the all-important advance. The downside of that number is that most if not all of it is recoupable against an artist's album sales, which are no longer what they used to be, meaning it's going to take that much longer to get in the black. But perhaps the problem is not with the label model overall, but just in the fact that no one's bothered to take a good, hard look at the way they have done business for the last few decades. Contracts written now are very similar to contracts written back in the '70s and '80s, despite new technology that makes certain provisions completely obsolete. It seems as though once a specific clause works its way into the contract, it's nearly impossible to delete it. Beyond that, a lot of standard business practice is hopelessly outdated, and almost bewildering to consider in the first place. Once upon a time, there was no way to reliably track album sales, so the charts used the information on how many albums were shipped to retailers to determine what record "sold" the most copies. This meant that labels had an incentive to ship more records, while retailers were more interested in not having to pay for product that wasn't going to move. It also meant that it was nearly impossible to tell what the artist was owed in royalties until the hard sales figures came back from the retailers at the end of the billing period. The solution was that retailers could send back product for a full refund, and record companies held in reserve a certain percentage of artist royalties owed on albums "sold," so that they weren't paying out on albums that ultimately didn't sell. Now, with ISRCs and other digital tracking information, there's no reason to ship excess albums to retailers to pump up sales figures. But the return policy is still in place, and, therefore, so is the provision in an artist's contracts that states that some of the artist's royalties will be held in reserve against future returns. This is one example of several that would seem equally ridiculous (although, to my mind, nothing tops the "packaging" deduction that in many cases is still applied to digital sales) but that persist because no one has bothered to take a hard look at them. Labels wouldn't, since these practices tend to benefit them, and most artists aren't in a position to argue contract points like that; even if they are, they might not know to look for them, or they might be told that it's simply part of "the cost of doing business," and nonnegotiable. The shifts in the industry have given labels the chance to reevaluate the way they sign and promote artists and how to make money, and the labels that are able to take advantage of this opportunity will be the ones that survive. What the digital revolution exposed is that labels were relying too heavily on album sales for revenue rather than looking for new revenue streams, and any investor will tell you that's a recipe for disaster.

The basic concept of a record label is not evil. The idea that a company will give bands the start-up capital needed to launch their careers is fairly reasonable and something that bands are still seeking today. The wording may have changed in that independent artists aren't talking about labels anymore as much as they're talking about good placements on television or corporate sponsorships, but the basic relationship is the same; artists want someone who can provide the money they need up front to get their career moving. As Damian Kulash pointed out in his February 2010 op-ed piece for the *New York Times*, there aren't any banks crazy enough to give business loans to musicians, no matter what kind of business plan they present. It's not an accident that, even as people have been talking about the death of the music industry overall and labels specifically since around 2001, there are still labels, and the biggest-selling artists are still signed to them. The good news for labels is that the move to digital has exposed the flaw in the way they do business and given them a chance to figure out exactly what they have to offer artists and what artists actually need from them. To a great extent, the problems the record industry is dealing with now had their start long before the first downloads started.

I got a chance to speak with Chris Arbisi, who had been with a band called White Trash in the early '90s, about the band's experience getting signed to a major label contract and what that involved. Chris told me that the band was signed to a publishing deal first, which led them to playing shows in New York City during the New Music Seminar in summer 1989. That winter they were signed to a deal with EMI to produce a four-song demo and video. The demo was sent to people and labels that might be interested in signing a group like White Trash in 1990, and in the spring the band signed a deal with Q Prime Management. Chris referred to this as "the fast track to getting an album deal." The album deal followed not long after, as Elektra picked them up and gave them $400,000 for their first album. Elektra also flew the band out to California for a couple of months to record the album, which was released in 1991 after which the band began touring. In 1992, Elektra was interested in a second album and offered them $200,000 for it, but internal problems in the band kept them from recording it. When I was talking to Chris about their experience, I commented on how different their deal was from the deals that are being offered to a lot of young bands now, and Chris admitted that the label spent a lot on a new band. He said, "We were getting full-page ads in *Billboard*, a full-page ad with Suzuki in *Entertainment Weekly* that mentioned our single. I don't think bands are getting that kind of treatment anymore. They put a lot of money into us, to fly us out to California to make the record. We could have made the record in New York, or they could have flown the engineer and producer out here instead of flying seven guys out there and putting them up in a hotel for a couple months, but that was the mind-set at the time."

This kind of financial hubris was common through the '90s, when the music business was booming, and that's why the state of labels was questionable before the CD sales slump began in earnest. The late '90s saw a trend of consolidation throughout the record industry leading to a situation where labels were disappearing regularly. By the time the banner CD sales year of 2000 rolled around, the industry was down to about five major labels controlling virtually all the popular music released in the US. A lot of the accounts of file sharing from the early days specifically mention the difficulty in finding any music beyond what was being played on the Top 40 stations, which causes many to be skeptical when record companies plead poverty as a reason for why they're not signing innovative bands lately. When the money was rolling in, all anyone wanted to do was find the next 'NSync. Now that the industry is seeing consistent drops in CD sales, their former main source of income, every year, they're busy trying to find the next Justin Bieber. It was in the late '90s that shorter contract lengths and increased emphasis on immediate hits began to emerge as well. After the 1999 Grammys, Sheryl Crow spoke about the trends in the music industry that had caused her original label to be shut down and why it was hurting music in general, pointing out that "they sign two-album deals now. I was signed to seven albums, and I was given a chance to get on the road and hone my craft. You want artists who have a strong point of view, who have the potential to grow into something wonderful, like Jackson Browne and Joni Mitchell, who found themselves by touring and continuing to write, and their album sales slowly grew. But now artists aren't getting that opportunity, because there's pressure to have instant hits."[24] The more you look at the music industry as it came into the digital distribution years, the

---

24 *Ripped: How the Wired Generation Revolutionized Music* by Greg Kot. Scribner, New York, 2009. Pg. 6

more it becomes apparent that the problems that were blamed on Napster weren't problems created by Napster, but rather that the rise of Napster exposed problems that had been simmering for the previous decade.

How are bands signed in the post-Napster years? My friend Matthew Taylor was a member of Moses Mayfield, an eclectic rock group out of Alabama who were signed to Universal between 2004 and 2007. I asked him a few questions about the band's experiences during that time and how they got noticed, to see how the business had changed from the days of Chris Arbisi. The beginning of their stories is close to the same; Moses Mayfield recorded a live DVD in Birmingham that they sent to their attorney in New York, who forwarded it to the top A&R representatives at major labels. Both White Trash and Moses Mayfield had part of their business team in place before they had a record contract; for White Trash it was the management company, and for Moses Mayfield it was their attorney. Moses Mayfield was approached by a talent evaluator at Epic, and ended up signing with the label. I asked Matt what concerns the band had about the contract offered them, and he said their concerns were typical: "Small royalties after the company recoups the advance, no mention of tour support. Though we started from a position of power (we were flown up to New York by the labels to perform a series of showcases), the contracts back then were very favorable to the labels."

Moses Mayfield got caught up in the tides of the larger business world, though, as Matthew explained that "when we first signed with Epic, our A&R guy was the president of A&R for the label, essentially the second in command. So they were very invested in our success—inclusion on a compilation CD circulated to the top one hundred radio stations in America, a guest spot on *The Hills*, and they even gave us more money for the recording. Things went wrong in the midst of our first national tour. The label was reluctant to give us tour support, so we raised money to rent a bus. In retrospect, this was only a prelude to the actual bombshell: our A&R guy had decided to switch to Columbia Records, and he expected us to make a decision the night that he told us this. Ultimately we followed our A&R guy (a decision I'm still not sure was the right one). The level of support instantly dropped, and it became more evident that Columbia was really just humoring us. We released our album March 27th of 2007 with little promotion. The next day our A&R rep left Sony/BMG entirely."[25] They ended up being dropped by Columbia later that year, and they broke up at the same time. In contrast to the experience of White Trash, Moses Mayfield's label put far less effort and money into promoting them, and where Elektra was willing to pay for a second album from White Trash even though the first album hadn't been a hit, Columbia wasn't interested at all in developing Moses Mayfield beyond their first album.

There are independent labels that have started to come up in the business, but it's worth noting that not every small or niche label is truly independent in the sense that they're unconnected to the major labels. There are a lot of very small labels that are either vanity labels started by artists or just labels attempting to capitalize on a niche market by using a different name but are still connected to major labels. Honestly, if you like the artist, this shouldn't make too much of a difference to you, but if you're interested in finding out which labels are self-contained and which are smaller offshoots of a major label, a quick Google search is usually enough to figure it out. Even then, the answer isn't necessarily straightforward, depending on how stringent you are on the definition of *independent*. Country star Jason Aldean is classified as an independent artist by *Billboard* and other industry outlets and is signed to an independent label, Broken Bow Records. If you want to get picky, though, Broken Bow Records has a distribution deal with RED Distribution, which is a sales and marketing division of Sony Music Entertainment. RED offers a lot of services that independent labels and bands find difficult to arrange on their own, and the roster of artists that they work with is an impressive list, including big names like Nine Inch Nails and MGMT as well as bands with smaller but incredibly dedicated

---

25 Columbia Records is owned by the Sony Music Group.

followings like Rodrigo y Gabriela, As I Lay Dying, and the controversial OFWGKTA. Most major labels have a distribution arm that will pick up work with independent labels or artists but aren't necessarily hands-on in terms of the creative end of things.

Mac Miller of Pennsylvania has been making news for his "independent" career and how he's selling out shows without radio or major label support, but he *is* signed to a label. Rostrum Records may not be a major label, or in any way connected to a major label, but they are a record label, and they are able to offer support and services to Mac Miller as part of their agreement, which keeps the artist from having to piece them together a la carte or (more likely) perform the tasks on his own. Rostrum Records is also not averse to partnering with major labels, since their star artist Wiz Khalifa is coproduced by Rostrum and Atlantic Records. With the support of Rostrum, Mac Miller was able to catapult his first album, *Blue Slide Park*, to a number-one debut on the *Billboard* 200 with 144,000 copies sold. This marked the first time since 1995 that an independently distributed debut album made hit number one. While some may see this as a meteoric rise to stardom, the truth is that Miller and Rostrum have been working separately and together for years to create names for themselves locally and nationally, and the success they're having now with *Blue Slide Park* comes out of those years of work, even if it seems like Miller has exploded out of nowhere. Miller's tours are geared toward under-twenty-one or all-ages clubs, because his team knows that most of his fans online are teenagers. Incentives were offered to fans to preorder the record, with special offers when certain preorder milestones were hit that encouraged fans not only to preorder for themselves but also to encourage their friends to do so. This is a fairly sophisticated and well-organized marketing and publicity effort, and proof that even independent labels can give artists a huge boost that might not be possible if they were working alone.

One of the biggest problems major labels have been struggling with since the early years of the 2000s is an image problem. There were several high-profile artists who went on the record as encouraging fans to download their albums, because they weren't going to see any money from the legitimate album sales anyway. While it seems impossible, most of them were probably right; the breakdown of where the money goes from an album sold is pretty heavily tipped in favor of the record company, and beyond that most record companies make it a policy to keep giving artists advances that are recoupable against future album sales rather than worrying about the nitty-gritty details of accounting to the artist for every single album sold. Some of this makes sense; there are a wide variety of categories and price points when it comes to how record labels handle album sales and what the company is owed for each particular sale. Aside from the somewhat obvious digital versus physical sales, there's full-price, mid-line, and budget categories as well as special categories for albums sold in military PXs. And that's just for US-based album sales; foreign sales have all of these categories plus the added issue of money due to the local distributor as well as special taxes or tariffs that may be due. Most artists signed to a major label contract were kept in a constant "unrecouped" state, meaning that since the record company had not made back their initial investment through royalties due to the artist, the artist's royalties went straight to the record company.

For a better explanation of how this happens, lets take a moment and look at how many albums the average first time artist would have to sell in order to get their account in the black. Taking the example used in chapter 6, we know that the cost to launch a new pop artist is generally a total of $1 million. The break down on that is a $200,000 advance, a $200,000 recording budget, three music videos budgeted at $200,000 total, tour support in the amount of $100,000, and promotion and marketing budgets that come to $300,000. Usually video costs are only 50 percent recoupable (i.e., the money the label spent is meant to be paid back by the artist) from the album sales, so we'll knock off $100,000, but everything else is generally fully recoupable from album sales, so we're still left with a $900,000 deficit. In the tenth edition of *This Business of Music*, the authors provide a breakdown of a $14.98 MSRP CD, which is still a fair price for CDs purchased physically. The artist's royalty on an album sale tends to be somewhere between 9 and 12 percent of the MSRP, so let's make the math easy and go with 10 percent. That means an artist looking over that contract would expect to earn about $1.50 per album sold, which doesn't sound so bad, and at that rate, they'd be able to recoup their album costs after selling six hundred thousand albums—rough, but not impossible. Before we get to that, though, there are some deductions taken off the top of that $14.98 for packaging (25 percent) and free goods given promotionally to retailers (15 percent). Take those off and we're looking at a 40 percent loss from the original $14.98, which means we're now working with $8.99 per album sold that the artist's percentage is calculated from. Ten percent of $8.99 is $0.89, so now the artist has to sell 1,011,235 albums in order to climb out of that $900,000 hole the labels dug for them. It will probably take a while to get there too, since the labels generally hold somewhere around 35 percent of an artist's album royalties in reserve against retailers returning unsold merchandise, so the artist wouldn't even be credited the full $0.89 for those first albums, since reserves are held and distributed in increments over the next several accounting periods. Which means that on the off chance an artist does sell over a million albums, the money from those albums won't be credited to their account for another two or three accounting periods, depending on the distribution schedule. This doesn't take into account whether or not important producers may have worked on the album, since those producers will likely also receive royalty percentage points, and those points come off the artist's side of the pie, not the label's side.

Readers who have some math skills may notice that while it may take over a million albums to earn back that $900,000 through artist royalties, the record company's cut would seem to be much more generous, and that it would have earned back that money with far fewer albums sold. If the artist is earning $0.89 per album after deductions, the record company is earning around $8.10 per album. This means that even if you look at that full $1 million initial investment, the company has earned their money back after 123,456 albums have been sold.[26] It takes almost a million more albums to get the artist's account in the black even after the record company has officially recouped all the money they spent in the first place. On the very slim chance this new artist (since we looked at the typical investment for a new artist) does sell those 1,011,235 albums to claw his or her way out of debt, the record company will have made $7,191,003.50 over their $1 million investment. I'm pretty certain no one is against a company turning a healthy profit for providing the many services most record companies do, but septupling your investment while telling the artist that they've just barely made back the money you spent on them does seem disingenuous at best, and just this side of evil at worst.

The problem here is that most albums never recoup their initial investment, and most artists never work their way out of debt to the record company. The absurd amount of money earned by the few artists who do manage to become big sellers makes up for the money invested in artists who never manage to earn back the money spent on them either through artist royalties or through the slice owed the record company. The easy answer here seems to be that record companies just shouldn't invest as heavily in new artists, but one of the complaints regarding the way record companies are currently run is that they're not willing to take a chance on new artists or give them the kind of support needed to really get their careers moving. The way record companies do business also supports many other people working behind the scenes in the music industry; recording engineers, studio musicians, local stagehands and electrical unions that work on concerts, entertainment attorneys, and other jobs too numerous to name that are essentially invisible to the average music fan, but which are all valuable

---

26 I swear I didn't make that number up. Go ahead and divide 1,000,000 by 8.1, and check for yourself if you don't believe me.

to the music industry overall. So the question becomes where the balance should be struck between giving artists the kind of investment they need to really get up and rolling, and controlling costs so that those same artists don't spend their entire careers in debt to their record companies. Perhaps major labels begin only catering to well-established artists, offering top-flight service to proven entities. Perhaps the industry will figure out a way to spend less money more effectively on new artists. Only time will tell.

Let's say that you've launched your career as an independent artist and have been successful enough to catch the eye of a record label, but not successful enough that you have someone well versed in music business around to act as a manager or agent. Chances are that if you're offered a contract, you'll end up negotiating it on your own, and unless you've got the time to read several very thick textbooks, you're going to be trying to read a document containing terms that you've never seen before and aren't likely to see again in any other context. There's a couple of tricks to learn here, which is that at the end of any contract there will be a section labeled "Definitions" that will spell out exactly what certain terms mean in the context of that contract. You should always read that section and refer to it as you're reading the rest of the contract. Now that you have a better grasp on what the contract says, you have to figure out if the terms are even slightly favorable for you. Shockingly enough, there's a website for that.

The unimaginatively named Moses Avalon Royalty Calculator[27] is a feature on Moses Avalon's website that lets you plug in various splits and percentages, so that you can figure out in practical terms exactly what the contract in front of you is offering. The website not only acts as a specialized calculator but also features a lot of information on what the terms mean and some information on what kind of numbers are typical for different kinds of royalties or percentages. Once you've entered all the information, you can enter in total number of albums sold to find out how much the artist will make, how much will be paid out in mechanical royalties, how much the

---

27 Found at http://www.mosesavalon.com/moses-avalon-royalty-calculator/.

producer will make, and how many records you have to sell to break even. While this website won't completely replace a trained entertainment attorney well versed in the music industry, it does help level the playing field for artists or managers who are less experienced with these kinds of negotiations. That's not to say that having consulted Moses Avalon's website will let you negotiate a perfect contract; as discussed previously, almost all label contracts are vastly more favorable to the label than to the artist, and most record companies aren't afraid of walking away from artists who push too hard for higher royalties or for dropping certain contract provisions. But at least you'll know what you're getting into and what chance you have of getting yourself out of the land of the unrecouped, and that's something that many artists in the past haven't known going into their contracts.

Lately there have been disputes between many small music-based start-ups and labels, most notably with streaming services. At the Digital Music Forum East held in New York in February 2012, Rhapsody VP and General Council Cecily Mak revealed the hurdles that are still in place when it comes to working with labels. "The bigger problem is getting the sound recording license in the first place. We had as recently as last week at SF MusicTech somebody from a major record label basically sit there and say publicly that to get that license from the major record label you need to bring significant advances [and] you need to give up equity in your company .... I could comment further on that but it's just a brutal, brutal reality for companies that want to do something really innovative and cool and come into market. And I think it's perhaps too significant of a barrier." As of right now, the labels have the power, because they control the rights to the biggest hits, the songs that people come to streaming services to hear. This could be part of the reason why Spotify seems to be engaged in endless rounds of fund-raising as it continues to launch in new territories; if they need to provide large, up-front payments to the labels to secure licenses for their catalog in each new country or territory they expand into, then whatever money they're taking in would be quickly depleted. The push to get all artists and their recordings on streaming services will come from fans and possibly from artists, but the labels will attempt to hold on to their control for as long as they can. This isn't particularly surprising, since it's what they've done with every jump forward in music technology, but it does mean that early innovators like Rhapsody will likely suffer more for paving the way than will later services, who will come into the business once streaming is more established and labels are less hostile. As streaming becomes more common and gains more habitual users, more labels will probably relax their standards on releasing music for streaming services.

The biggest question is what can labels offer their clients that can't be found elsewhere, especially as other business interests get involved in the music game. There are always going to be artists who aren't up to the task of managing their own careers, and for those artists the oversight of a label can be valuable in its own right, but what's to stop artists from hiring independent music professionals to oversee their business and leaving behind the mass of contracts, restrictions, and royalty cuts that come with record contracts? For some, the feeling that they're being taken care of by a company with a big name and a good reputation is what they want, and they're willing to sacrifice a certain amount of control and income in order to make that happen. For now, labels still have the money to back artists in a way that most artists can't achieve independently, especially at the beginning of their careers, but how long will that last? Record companies were built on revenue made from music sales, and the numbers just aren't going to be what they were anymore.

CHAPTER 11:

THE NEW MEASURE OF A SUPERSTAR

One of the best ways to understand that labels, if not as healthy as they once were, are still a force to be reckoned with, comes when you take a look at current superstars. Despite financial hardships facing the industry's distribution arm, artists such as Lady Gaga, Rihanna, Justin Bieber, Nickelback, Katy Perry, and others are still able to move huge amounts of music and create concerts that cost in the hundreds of thousands, if not millions, just to stage once, never mind take on a world-wide tour. Yet somehow these artists exist, even thrive, and sell out arenas across the globe. Lady Gaga's "Monster's Ball" tour is the highest-grossing tour ever by a debut headlining artist and took a huge investment on the part of a label. But to say that only these big-name, headlining acts can be considered superstars in this day and age overlooks the new ways that artists are making their mark on the world.

One of the biggest changes that the music industry has seen in the last decade or so is, of course, the drastic slide in album sales. The year 2000 saw more than 943 million albums sold in the US. However, Napster had launched in 1999, and 2000 saw it gain enough ground so that 2001 was the year when the music industry started to feel the pinch of peer-to-peer networks in their sales data in high-enough numbers to begin pursuing legal action against the creators and users of such sites. Because of this, 2000 ended up as the peak year for album sales. The top-selling album of 2000 was 'N Sync's *No Strings Attached*, which is not a surprise to anyone who remembers the inescapability of such singles as "Bye Bye Bye" and "It's Gonna Be Me" at the time. Not only was it the top-selling album of the year, but it also still holds the title of fastest-selling album of all time after selling over two million units and being certified double platinum within its first week of sales. The total for the year would be within spitting distance of 10 million units in the US, with over 11 million sold worldwide. Compare that to the year 2010, when the top-selling album was Eminem's *Recovery*, which ended up selling a total of 3.42 million copies. Total album sales for 2010 were 326.2 million units. In the span of a decade, album sales had slumped by 65 percent overall. Frankly, there's no reason to expect that this is going to change, and reading the same article that wrings its hands over slumping album sales every year for the past decade is getting tedious.

These numbers aren't just interesting for what they tell us about current album sales but also for what they tell us about the people buying those albums. Eminem's album was notable not only for being the top-selling album for 2010 but also for being his sixth number-one album in a row, beginning with 1999's *The Slim Shady* LP. Compared to the other releases, *Recovery* has performed well but not spectacularly for Eminem. Its sales in the year of release topped 2009's *Relapse* but fell far short of the numbers put up by *Encore* (2004), *The Eminem Show* (2002), the *Marshal Mathers* LP (2000), and *The Slim Shady* LP. It does speak to the fact that Eminem's fan base has stayed fairly loyal over the last decade, which has allowed him to count on a certain amount of album sales as a matter of course. *Recovery* was also the top-selling digital album of 2010, with 852,000 downloads, and the single "Love the Way You Lie" was the number three downloaded single of the year, with 4.25 million downloads. So while Eminem's album sales have remained strong in the past twelve years of his career, even he is facing the fact that single sales may be the new arbiter of success in the digital age.

The proof of this new form of success is discovered in Katy Perry, whose sophomore album *Teenage Dream* put up unsubstantial numbers in its initial release, but ended up making history, as she had a fifth single from the album that hit *Billboard*'s Hot 100 in 2011, which makes six total singles of hers that have performed that feat. There are only seven artists who have had five or more consecutive singles hit number one; Perry's company includes Elvis Presley, the Beatles, Michael Jackson, and Mariah Carey. Moreover, Perry is the first female artist and second artist overall to have five songs from one album hit number one. The first was Michael Jackson. This is becoming old hat for Perry, who also landed the top single of the year for 2010 in terms of sales. "California Gurls" sold 4.4 million downloads, putting it ahead of such powerhouses as Train's "Soul Sister" and Eminem's "Love the Way You Lie." Those who were quick to dismiss Perry as a flash in the pan when "I Kissed a Girl" hit have been proven wrong, as she continues to dominate the airwaves and sales charts even if there has been scant critical acclaim for her work. The number of hits off *Teenage Dream* has also helped to fuel continuing sales for the album. After all, with the current $1.29 pricing for singles on iTunes, it doesn't take too long before it seems economical to just buy the whole album rather than continuing to purchase songs individually. iTunes makes this especially attractive by tracking what songs you've already purchased from an album and letting you "complete" the album, with the deduction for that first single (or first two or three singles) deducted from the total album cost. Perry may not be changing the face of pop music, but she is making history by maintaining a commitment to catchy crowd-pleasing singles that are radio-friendly. *Teenage Dream* climbed from its first week sales of 192,000 in August 2010 to being certified double platinum on June 15, 2012. The album (original and re-release) spent ninety-five weeks on the *Billboard* 200 chart. Whereas other popular artists released several albums over the same length of time, each with one or two hits apiece, Perry rode one album for nearly two years on the strength of a series of singles. It's an intriguing model for those in the business and those looking to get into the business, and one that could prove more realistic in the digital-download world.

Given the impressive decline in album sales, it's worthwhile to examine other measures of success for artists aside from sales figures. One technique that has worked well for some groups that could best be described as "alternative" is relying on touring for the majority of their revenue. This technique has worked well for My Morning Jacket, a band whose most recent album, Circuital, is their best performing album so far, hitting number five on the US album charts. Despite unimpressive sales, they sold out their 2008 show at New York's Radio City Music hall in under twenty-two minutes. They're continuing a tradition that's been around for decades, as Phish fans can attest, but the fact that the touring heavy jam band model continues to work into the digital age is something that not many would have predicted. Though there are clear indications that in this digital age with auto-tune running rampant through most of the top pop singles, some people are more appreciative of concerts that feature bands who can play their own instruments and sing live without mechanical assistance. This model also rewards bands that are able to give fans a different experience than they would have just listening to the album or watching the music videos in their own home. Lady Gaga's record-breaking Monster's Ball tour is well known for featuring different arrangements of her top hits that feature Gaga's voice and piano-playing ability to their full extent as well as a mind-bending array of costumes, sets, choreography, and other elements that make it well worth the money for her legions of fans to go see her.

Of course, even in the touring world, there aren't many surprises. The ten top-earning concerts of August 2011 have four spots taken up by shows on Paul McCartney's tour, and Taylor Swift holds another three. Towards the end of summer, Bon Jovi also emerged as a huge seller on the concert circuit. Two of these three artists are legacy acts and have fans spanning generations. An analysis of the top-grossing tour acts of the past decade conducted by Deloitte in August 2011 found that 94 percent of the top touring artists were over the age of forty. More specifically, they have a large number of fans who are in an age bracket where they likely have more disposable income to spend on things like concerts. By and large, the best-selling tours are the ones that appeal to two very different demographics: young teenagers, and adults in their late thirties to sixties. The reason those two groups are the biggest spenders is the same: the person actually spending the money tends to be an adult with a stable job. Young teenagers are still living at home, and more often then not it's their parents who are paying for concert tickets, album downloads, T-shirts, and whatever other products you can slap an artist's face onto. This same generalization applies to adults who have moved out of the time of their life spent in college, grad school, or low-paying entry-level positions; they've got a little more money to spend and tend to be past the age where they want to sit in the nosebleed sections, so they're willing to spend the money on good seats for bands that they enjoy if they know the show will be worth their time. There is also the theory that younger acts are touring in conjunction with festivals rather than as independent entities, which could affect how their numbers are perceived (it's hard to determine how many people who went to Coachella saw any one band in particular), and that in the future we'll see more of these groups striking out on their own as they grow an audience. It could be, though, that younger fans enjoy the festival experience more. While fans of Bon Jovi may be past the days of spending twelve hours in the sun listening to music, standing in line for porta-potties, and paying ten dollars for a cheeseburger, festivals like Bonnaroo, Coachella, and Ultra have been gaining in popularity with younger fans, and there are smaller festivals springing up across the country. While there are some contemporary superstars capable of selling out stadiums on their own, dismissing the artists who headline on big festivals for lack of a solo tour is shortsighted.

Tours may be good moneymakers, though not every artist is made for the stage. It's been said for a long time that there's no such thing as bad publicity; the Internet seems to have gone out of its way to test this theory. The case of Lana Del Rey is a good example; while she had a small following based on some YouTube videos she'd released of singles off her album *Born to Die* months before the album was released, the buzz around her really grew after she performed on *Saturday Night Live* in early January 2012 in a performance that even her fans were hard-pressed to defend. While Del Rey's performance wasn't on the level of the Ashley Simpson incident on the same show, the singer's demeanor and body language made it clear that she wasn't comfortable or confident in front of an audience. Overnight, *Lana Del Rey* became one of the most-searched terms on the Internet, and people who had never heard of her before all of a sudden had fully formed opinions that they took to the Internet to share with millions around the world. The debate raged: Was she a talented artist thrust into a performance she wasn't ready for, or was she a pretty girl sold on the value of her good looks and mildly provocative "character" who possessed no particular musical talent of any kind? In most of these arguments, the term *hipster* was tossed around a lot, usually derisively, but a lot of people also started looking up her videos and her music on Spotify to better arm themselves for whichever side of the debate they planted themselves on. When the album *Born to Die* was released a couple of weeks after the infamous *Saturday Night Live* performance, it catapulted to number two on the *Billboard* 200 albums chart. Not bad for an album that was, when all was said and done, reviewed as pretty firmly middle-of-the-road pop. Two solid weeks' worth of debate over whether their star had gotten lip injections and what that said about her as a person probably wasn't the goal that Interscope records was looking for when she was booked on *Saturday Night Live*, but I'm sure they weren't disappointed with the outcome either, since it resulted in record sales and a high-profile debut for *Born to Die*. In fact, the video of her *Saturday Night Live* performance has been posted to the official Lana Del Rey Vevo channel.

Clearly whatever embarrassment Del Rey suffered was fine with Interscope, as long as it got her name on more lips.

One of the changes that the industry has gone through with regard to superstar artists has been largely hidden from the public and is still shrouded in a certain amount of mystery is the so-called 360 contract. By the most basic of explanations, a 360 contract (or "multiple rights" contract) is one that grants the record company a share of profits from business ventures above and beyond record sales and licensing. The earliest version that's been reported is from 2002 and was between Robbie Williams and EMI, but since then they've become more common at both major labels and some independent labels. The theory behind them is that because the record label invests the time and advertising dollars necessary to bring an act to public attention and adoration, then they should get a share of any income generated by that act whether it's directly related to record sales or not. It's not a bad theory, and something the labels probably should have thought about long before record sales started declining, since almost every child over the age of five has heard all the typical admonishments against putting all your eggs in a single basket. There are a lot of arguments for and against the deals, coming from the sources you'd suspect; record labels say that the deals come with larger up-front payments and an increased investment in the band from the record company because of the potential for larger payouts. That is, they're more willing to work with you to make you happen because they know that there's more money in it for them if you do. That is, because the record label is being reimbursed through a variety of streams, they will put more effort into developing a band holistically instead of just focusing on the first single, and then quickly losing interest in the band once the initial flush of attention has passed. On the other side, there's skepticism that a 360 contract would convince a label to keep an act that was faltering and the balking at signing over more rights to a record label. Revenue streams that have traditionally been mostly left up to artists like merchandise and touring have become large moneymakers for many groups that never saw a dime of royalties from their labels due to un-recouped accounts, so it's understandable that many groups would be hesitant to surrender any of that money to labels. If a band is approached by a label that wants to sign them to one of these contracts, there's no one right answer or one wrong answer that they can give; it's just a matter of determining what you're willing to give up and what you'll be getting in return. For superstars like Madonna, there's very little risk to her, because her wealth should be secure at this point, so giving up pieces of touring, merchandise, and other income streams to LiveNation in exchange for a large up-front payment and intense promotion makes sense. For a band that's just starting out, it might not. While a 360 contract may convince record labels to put more time into development, we're at a point in our culture where audiences are moving from one thing to the next faster than ever. The Internet and reality TV has shortened our attention span, so now there's the potential that it's not just the label that will ignore you if your first hit doesn't make it, it's the other tastemakers out there. Any band that's approached with one of these contracts is going to have the make the call themselves, and if you've developed yourselves well independently, you hopefully have a good idea of the kind of audience appeal you'll have after transitioning to a major label and if the sort of amplification that they can offer is going to boost your career or give you a very large stage to fizzle out on.

We may be in the waning days of the true superstars. It's hard to say what kind of devotion fans will have to acts when hundreds, if not thousands, of artists put their music out on the Internet every single day and a significant portion of the music fan culture has become obsessed with being onto the next thing even as whatever they were fans of last week just broke a million YouTube hits or one hundred thousand Facebook fans. Every generation thinks that the younger generations are Doing It Wrong, but the fact of the matter is the immediacy of the Internet has had an effect on our cultural attentions, not just in music but in movies, news, and almost every other facet of culture. Part of the reason the album format may be on the way out is not that it's not worthwhile to put together a well-thought-out and artistically beautiful album anymore, because if you take too long putting the album together, the world may move on without you. I'm very interested to see what happens to the superstars of the aughts as time goes by; there are only a few I would say have any real staying power. But then again, I doubt anyone in 1998 would have told you that out of all the boy-band members floating around, it was Justin Timberlake who would go the distance.

Labels will always exist in some form or another, but the shift in the music marketplace since the development of the Internet will change the way they do business. Some existing labels will be able to adapt, and some won't, but consolidating many artists under one roof offering business services just makes more sense logically and financially than each and every artist basically creating their own whole company to manage their career. Labels still have a lot to offer artists, and while they may change drastically, I don't see a future without some kind of record-label-like structure available for artists interested in that business model.

CHAPTER 12:

YOU GIVE LOVE A BAD NAME: COPYRIGHT OR COPYWRONG

However you feel about copyright law, it's best to be well informed about what protections it does and doesn't offer and to have a basic idea of how the permissions associated with copyright law work. There's a lot of misconceptions and urban myths out there about what copyright is, how it's enforced, and what enforcement means. Beyond that, there's even further confusion, or just flat-out ignorance, of other areas of copyright law that are important for musicians and consumers to be aware of (what is public domain, and how do I know if a song is in the public domain or not,; what's considered fair use; when do you have to get a license for using a song, and more). Picking up a book on copyright isn't a terrible idea for musicians interested in recording and selling their own music, or for anyone who wants to make money from creative endeavors. Knowing what your rights are as a creator is important, and it's good to have a reference around. This chapter will cover some basics of copyright and address what it does and doesn't mean for independent artists.

First of all, let's address what copyright really is; it is, quite literally, the right to make, distribute, and profit from copies of your work. Copyright is not something that needs to be granted by the government; it is inherent in the work once it is in a fixed medium. So, you can't copyright an idea you have in your head, but once you write that idea down or record it somehow, the copyright goes into effect immediately. The federal copyright office handles registration of copyrights. Registration is not necessary for copyright protection, but it is useful should you become involved in an infringement case. Also, being granted a registration from the copyright office doesn't mean that a work is not infringing on another copyrighted work; they don't check to see if your work or if anyone else's work has any similarity to other copyrighted works. It's really just a kind of rubber stamp that affirms that you've claimed copyright in a work and registered it with the copyright office on that particular date. Should you choose not to register your copyright, it's a good idea to have dated copies of your workbooks, early recordings, or notes in your calendar detailing the creative process that led to new songs and recordings, just in case. It's not frequent that an independent artist is infringed upon, but it can happen, and having proof that your song existed on such-and-such a date, even if it was not registered with the copyright office, can make a big difference.

If you're writing songs, one of the first steps you should take in your career is to register yourself with a performing rights organization. These organizations will collect public performance royalties on your behalf from radio stations and anywhere that music is played for the enjoyment of the public. There are three major performing rights organizations (PROs) in the United States; they are ASCAP (the American Society of Composers, Authors, and Publishers), BMI (Broadcast Music Incorporated), and SESAC (the Society of European Stage Authors and Composers, which, despite the full name, does now represent mostly American songwriters). The largest difference between the three is that SESAC requires an application for membership to be approved and operates on a for-profit basis, whereas

ASCAP and BMI both offer open membership and operate as not-for-profit businesses. All of them operate the same way; they charge fees to venues that will be playing music in a public performance capacity in exchange for use of their catalog in the venue as the proprietor sees fit. They also handle performance royalties that are due to songwriters for songs played on the radio. The fees are then distributed to the songwriters registered with that PRO on the basis of play volume as estimated by the administration, with an administration fee deducted from artist with ASCAP or BMI and with an undisclosed extra amount deducted from the royalties of the artists with SESAC.

There's a separate entity, called SoundExchange, charged with collecting digital royalties, so no matter which PRO you sign up with, you should also be sure to register yourself with SoundExchange to ensure that your digital royalties are accounted to you. Digital-performance royalties are collected from a handful of sources, such digital cable and satellite television services, webcasts or streaming radio programs that are non-interactive (you can't select a playlist), and satellite radio stations. Unlike the PROs, which collect only performance royalties due to songwriters, SoundExchange collects royalties to the recording artist and the copyright holder of the sound recording. So, even if you didn't write the song, you'll still be eligible to collect digital royalties for it. It's an important step to remember if your music has a chance of being played by one of those outlets. Registering is free and requires US-based artists only to submit their information and a W-9. An administration fee is charged against royalties collected, though SoundExchange's website claims that this fee is "as low as possible." Some digital broadcasting services are handling their royalties directly rather than going through SoundExchange, but registering with them will ensure that all your bases are covered.

One of the things many people may not realize about copyright is that what you can and can't control changes once you distribute your work to the public. Until you distribute your work, you control everything about it and can sue anyone who infringes on your copyrighted work in any way. Once your work is distributed, there are some provisions that kick in that mean that a person who wants to create a version of your copyrighted song can do so without your permission if they follow specific accounting and creative guidelines. Alternately, you can create versions of another individual's copyrighted work and make them available for sale without actually violating copyright laws as long as you follow specific accounting and creative guidelines. This provision was actually put in place many, many years ago, in the days of player pianos, when it appeared that the Aeolian player-piano company had a monopoly on songs produced as player-piano scrolls. Because of this, the license to reproduce the copyrighted work of another individual for public distribution and sale is known as a mechanical license, even though these days there's nothing mechanical about it, as mentioned in chapter 2. When you refuse to negotiate a contract for a mechanical license, the individual (or you, if you're looking to do a cover song and haven't received permission to do so) can take out a compulsory mechanical license. Be warned, though, that compulsory mechanicals are generally not used in the industry because the accounting is incredibly complicated (you have to account monthly to the copyright holder), and by and large a compulsory mechanical license is more expensive, since you'll be required to pay the copyright holder the full statutory mechanical rate as dictated by law. As of the time of writing, that rate is 9.1¢ per song or 1.75¢ per minute of playing time or fraction thereof (whichever is greater) per copy sold.[28]

What happens if another artist wants to make a cover of your song? Well, obviously the first thing that will matter is if the artist is also independent or a signed artist. If it's the latter, you probably won't see that 9.1¢ or more per copy of the song sold when all is said and done. Standard

---

28 For the curious, this is a reason why there aren't many popular songs over five minutes long; over five minutes, and the 1.75¢ rate becomes more than the flat rate (10.5¢ versus 9.1¢, for those of you wondering) so record labels strongly discourage songs over five minutes because they don't want to pay the extra royalties on them.

industry practice for record labels is to negotiate with artists or other labels to get the statutory rate down to 75 percent of the applicable rate, which would be 6.825¢ for songs under five minutes and variable for songs over five minutes. Some high-profile or extremely successful artists will always be paid the statutory rate for their songs, but for smaller artists or writers, the rate will usually be negotiated down in the licensing process. After all, if you put your foot down for 9.1¢ in full, they could just choose not to use your song, and then you won't earn any money. If another independent artist wants to cover your song, obviously the two of you can work out a negotiated rate if the statutory rate is beyond their means.

If you want to do a cover song of a work that is still under copyright protection, you can purchase mechanical licenses fairly easily in most cases, since many songs are available for licensing through the Harry Fox agency, which has a website that can be navigated by independent artists without the help of a publishing firm, manager, or record label. In these cases you'll still have to pay the full statutory rate for the song. If you don't plan on selling more than 2,500 copies of the cover song, you'll pay for the licenses up front and won't have to do any accounting to Harry Fox for the licenses. If you're anticipating selling over 2,500 copies of the cover song, you'll have to pay quarterly royalties by a specific date or be subject to late fees and in some cases legal action. The Harry Fox website not only provides a way for independent artists to license music but also is very comprehensive in terms of the information they have about licensing and what licenses are necessary for certain uses. For example, it's important to remember that purchasing a mechanical license from Harry Fox entitles you to record and distribute only your version of a song. You can't then license that cover song to be used in a movie, commercial, or television show without further negotiations with the original song's publisher for a synchronization license. Performance rights are another thing to keep in mind; most venues that regularly hold performances have what's called a blanket license from one of the major PROs, which means that songs that are represented by those agencies are all allowed to be played in those venues without additional fees. To be on the safe side, though, for any public performances, you should check with the venue to see which agencies they have blanket licenses with and make sure that any cover songs you plan to perform are represented by the agency or agencies that have licenses with the venue.

Any song that you can't find through the Harry Fox agency might still be able to be licensed so you can record and sell a cover of it, but you'll just have to contact the publisher directly. To find the publisher, you can search for the song on the websites of ASCAP, BMI, or SESAC, and they should provide information on the song, its writers, and the publishing company or copyright administrator. However, getting in touch with the publisher and attempting to negotiate a license on your own is going to require a certain level of legal knowledge, and that's if you can get your phone calls returned. There are also artists whose songs are simply not covered because their publishing company or the artists themselves are not interested in covers or uncooperative. If you have a dream of building your album around a brilliant cover of a Prince song, you should probably find a new dream. You can still perform Prince covers in venues that have a blanket license for public performances as mentioned above, but you won't be able to get a mechanical license to record and sell your version of Prince's song. You can go compulsory, but it's widely acknowledged that those requirements are practically impossible even for large companies with their own accounting departments who are dedicated to tracking royalties and album sales. An independent artist doesn't stand a chance.

Another option if you're interested in doing creative cover songs that involves less worries about royalties but a little more research is to cover songs that are public-domain works. *Public domain* is a term for works that have never been under copyright protection or works that have had their copyright protection lapse. Most of these are older works from the 1920s or earlier, though some of them will date up to 1976, when the Copyright Reform Act removed the requirement that copyrighted works carry a ©

symbol in order to be considered under copyright protection. Occasionally, the symbol got left off, and the work entered public domain as soon as it was made available to the public. People make assumptions about public domain a lot, but it's best to do your research into what is or isn't public domain before using a particular piece of music, image, or what have you, because lawsuits are far more expensive than licenses. I remember one time when a character on the show *Glee* referred to a Madonna song as "public domain" when they meant that the other character had no right to keep the glee club from performing a Madonna song. Madonna songs are not in the public domain. That is not what *public domain* means. To find out if a song is public domain, the best thing to do is to check.

People also like to make assumptions about fair use, and the downside of fair use assumptions is that there are no hard-and-fast rules about what constitutes fair use; in an infringement defense, "fair use" must be tested by the courts in each individual case in order to determine whether or not that particular use qualifies. There are some guidelines that have been gained from previous court cases, but again, there's no guarantee that the decision would go the same way in a different case arguing the same defense. There have been some very famous fair-use cases that led people to inaccurate conclusions about the fair-use doctrine and what falls under its cover. When 2 Live Crew released the song "Pretty Woman" that was heavily based on and parodied Roy Orbison's "Oh, Pretty Woman," 2 Live Crew's manager had actually attempted to secure a license but was refused one by Acuff-Rose Music (the company that administrated the copyright for Orbison's "Oh, Pretty Woman"). The band went ahead with their version anyway and was taken to court by Acuff-Rose. The Supreme Court eventually ruled in favor of 2 Live Crew, stating that the song was obviously a parody and that its financial success didn't violate the fair-use clause of the copyright code. This does not mean that all parody versions of songs are considered fair use. In fact, when determining fair use, there are four factors that the courts consider. These factors, as found in section §107 of the copyright code, are

1. the purpose and character of the use, including whether such use is of a commercial nature or is for nonprofit educational purposes;
2. the nature of the copyrighted work;
3. the amount and substantiality of the portion used in relation to the copyrighted work as a whole; and
4. the effect of the use upon the potential market for or value of the copyrighted work.

Best practice is just to obtain a license for any copyrighted song if you intend to use the lyrics or tune in your song and are clearly intending to reference the original song. Infringement cases are expensive and can drag on for years. "Pretty Woman" was released in 1989. The Supreme Court verdict was handed down in 1994. Had the case gone against 2 Live Crew, not only would they have been out the money it cost them to bring the case all the way to the Supreme Court and the money that Acuff-Rose had sued for, but that's also five years' worth of accounting that would have had to be meticulously combed through in order to properly account to Acuff-Rose the mechanicals earned during that period. Acuff-Rose and 2 Live Crew officially settled out of court once the Supreme Court reversed the ruling by the Court of Appeals, and the terms of the settlement are not known, aside from the fact that the use of "Oh, Pretty Woman" was officially licensed by 2 Live Crew at the time of the settlement.

Even uses that would seem to fall well within fair-use guidelines should be closely examined. While there's an exception for educational use, more and more schools or other educational organizations are recording band concerts or marching band performances to sell, and once you make the decision to sell a video or CD of a performance, you need to obtain a mechanical license to make a CD or synchronization license *and* a mechanical license to sell videotaped performances that include copyrighted material. Even if the plan is just to sell CDs, the seller could still be held accountable for acquiring a mechanical license in order to produce copies of a copyrighted work. Schools could also be asked to pay a fee if they're charging for concert tickets. Most publishers will offer a discount or even free licenses for educational organizations that request licenses, but the point is that the license has to be secured to avoid the possibility of a lawsuit.

These regulations all apply to whole songs. Samples or pieces of an original composition, original recording, or both that are used in a new song are an area of copyright law that isn't explicitly covered by existing regulations. Any and all samples are negotiated individually, which means there's no statutory rate, so record labels or publishers are free to ask whatever rate they want, and using a sample that hasn't been licensed (or cleared) can result in a lawsuit. The price for samples will range wildly, depending on how popular the song or recording is, how much will be used, how it will be used, and how prominent the sample will be in the finished song. Sometimes a publisher will demand that the songwriter get a writing credit on the new song before granting rights to use a sample. Despite this, there's been a growing number of artists who work almost exclusively with prerecorded material (usually mashup artists or professional DJs), and some of them have even sold recordings. You may be asking how this is possible. The simple answer is that by-and-large, these artists don't seek licenses and just keep their fingers crossed that they don't get sued. Live performances of these works are usually covered by blanket performances licenses that will cover all the disparate songs that make up the new work. The same goes with playing these recordings on the radio; because airwaves are covered by blanket performance licenses, the use of all those songs in broadcast is allowed, whether they're played in full or as part of a new song. If you want to use a sample, and it's absolutely vital to the song in question, the simple answer is to not sell the recording. You can perform it, you can have it played on the radio, but once you try to sell it, you venture into legal hot water. Leave that for a time when your band (hopefully) becomes successful enough to pay the license fee. You could even use it as a fund-raising point for fans if it becomes popular at performances, a sort of "Hey, contribute to our band so that we can give you the recording you want!" pitch. Because this is such a popular area of music, the industry may one day catch up to what artists are already doing and what fans want, but until then, it's best to stay within legal bounds in order to avoid unnecessary expenses and conflict.

One of the most important things about copyright that is applicable to all musicians who may participate in a recording session, not just artists recording their own work, is that right now in the US, the copyright in sound recordings is something of an untested area. The copyright office sets out firm standards for what creative works can be designated "works made for hire" where the copyright in the work would be owned by the commissioner of the work rather than the creator of the work. Sound recordings are actually not included on the list of works that can be considered works made for hire. Despite this, anyone other than the artist who participates in a recording session is asked to sign a contract that designates the resulting composition as a work made for hire. What does this mean for you if you're not a lead artist on a recording? Well, at the moment it means that when you work recording sessions, you sign a piece of paper stating that since this is a work made for hire, you retain no rights to the finished product that you are producing, but *if at some point* it is deemed that this is not subject to the work-made-for-hire exception, you forfeit all your rights to the work and any possible future royalties. Bit of a tall order, considering how much money some recordings go on to make. In fact, this piece of paper is of questionable legality and persists only because no one has bothered to challenge the idea in court that a master recording is a work made for hire. Yet.

With the new regulations allowing recapturing of copyrights for artists who signed their copyrights over for the life of the copyright, that day may come very soon. It's not just background singers and studio musicians who are a threat in this case, either; it's entirely possible that music engineers, mixers, and producers who do not have their name on a recording's official copyright may challenge the ruling on the basis that their contribution should grant them a share of authorship in the work. And with the increasing use of electronic manipulation in recordings, it's hard to say that those contributions are inconsequential to the finished work or are not part of the creative process.

Obviously there's a lot of protection copyright can offer for songwriters and musicians. Even if you would like your music to be used creatively by other artists, you may not approve all the ways someone would want to use your song. For example, without copyright protection, your song could be used in a movie produced by a group of Nazis, and you wouldn't be able to do anything about it. Despite the fact that you never intended your song to be a message of racial intolerance and you personally do not subscribe to the viewpoints exhibited in the film, there would be no legal recourse you could seek against the filmmakers, and you could experience a serious blow to your personal and professional reputation. With copyright law, those Nazis would have to ask permission to use your song in their film, and if they didn't, you could sue them for everything they were worth. (Probably not much, since I don't think the Nazis are pulling down serious cash these days, but it's more about reputation than money in cases like that.) That's for synchronization licenses, though there have been some cases of political campaigns using songs at rallies that the specific artists had not specifically granted permission for and incurring the wrath of the songwriter or performer in the process. Unfortunately, if the venue the political rally takes place at has purchased a blanket public-performance license from the PRO that represents the songwriter's material, there's not much that the songwriter can do except make it clear to the public that she or he in no way supports or endorses that particular politician or political party. Unless, of course, they do, and then they're free to make that clear as well.

One of the options available to independent artists who want to make their work available for other people to exploit within specific circumstances but who don't necessarily have the time, energy, or expertise to evaluate and negotiate specific uses, is to use one of the six standard licenses offered by Creative Commons at their website, creativecommons.org. The licenses range from most restrictive to least restrictive and have written explanations in both normal human and legalese for your convenience. The most restrictive license allows others only to download and share your works as long as they credit you, but your work cannot be changed in any way, and it cannot be used commercially. The least restrictive license allows others to distribute, change, build upon, and use your work commercially as long as they credit you with the original creation. Within the other four licenses, you have options about commercial use and whether your work can be changed. Two of them require anyone using your work in their new creation to make their own work available under the same license, as under a "share alike" clause. There's also an option to waive all rights and place a work in the public domain immediately if the artist is not interested in retaining any rights to the work, including attribution, at all. These licenses are already in widespread use on sites such as Flickr, and the Internet giant Wikipedia uses the Attribution/Share-Alike license. The licenses also make your work searchable as something licensed by Creative Commons.

There are people who are moving toward copyright being used to allow more use and access rather than a means to restrict usage unless otherwise noted. Several websites now allow users to preemptively submit a Creative Commons license that will stipulate which uses are allowed, whether they expect a fee, and how they would like their work to be attributed. The argument is that by taking a step back from the "all rights reserved" format that copyrights have been in up until now, one can work to foster creativity and collaboration rather than tying people up with contracts, legalities, and negotiations. While this is true, it's also worthwhile to note that copyright law did not arise from a vacuum, and the reasons artists have needed special laws to protect their work for centuries is because there are many people who are all too eager to make money off work that isn't theirs without bothering to attribute or account to the original artist. I can't say that I'm entirely unbiased; I've been writing online for several years now, and if I found out that someone was using my words on their site without linking back to mine or acknowledging that the work was mine in some way, I'd be pretty angry. However, claiming and enforcing copyright in your work doesn't mean you can't give away your own work for free. As long as you're producing and selling your own work, it's up to you how you choose to make that work available to the public, and you're welcome to offer free downloads or pay-what-you-want downloads on your own website. Claiming copyright (or, more properly, enforcing copyright, since as previously mentioned, copyright is now considered to be inherent in a creative work once it's in a fixed medium) just means that you can choose whether other people can use your work and how you want to be compensated and acknowledged for those uses.

Copyright has gotten a bad name, with high-profile copyright infringement cases against average music consumers making the news as the RIAA did their best to stamp out illegal downloading. This is obviously not the case, and it's up to each individual artist how to handle copyright.

CHAPTER 13:

FAILURE IS ALWAYS AN OPTION AND OTHER THINGS YOU DON'T WANT TO HEAR

In the movies, hard work, perseverance in the face of adversity, and a twinkly smile are all you need to be handed whatever success you seek on a platter. Talent and hard work win out, the good guy gets the girl, and everyone goes home happy with lots of valuable life lessons in their pocket. In the real world, most people know that this isn't the case, but it's still hard to hear that it's not the case for you specifically. You're not like those people who fail! You're better! You've got great ideas, you work hard, you stay up late to write songs and learn chords, and you've put all your heart and soul into your music! You've even studied up and organized your business plan so that you look polished and professional and not like every other person out there recording songs in their basement and throwing them up on YouTube. There's no way you can fail! So what happens when you do?

According to the US Small Business Association, seven out of ten new businesses survive at least two years, and half at least five years. That rate is likely significantly lower for bands, though there are not as many hard numbers on them because bands can form, break up, and form again without ever filing any kind of official paperwork. Some of the inevitable failures can indeed be tracked to this sort of lack of effort; all you have to do to say you're in a band is find two or three other people who are willing to play instruments with you at roughly the same time. If you're a cover band, you don't even need to write your own music, and many "bands" see actual public performances or recordings as entirely unnecessary to their particular business venture. Even if you want to get a bit more organized, a lot of the initial steps are pretty easy. Starting a Facebook page or twitter isn't difficult, and registering for Bandcamp isn't particularly taxing either. Most of setting up a band online with various social-media outlets is the work of only a few very motivated hours, and a lot of projects that start enthusiastically end up running out of steam when it comes to doing the actual day in, day out work of updating, creating new material, rehearsing, and finding opportunities for performing.

One of the things that leads a lot of bands to fail is the expectation that what they're doing will always be fun. While a lot of the things one does in a band are fun, rehearsing a song to the point where it sounds good and you can play it without thinking every note through takes a lot of time and effort. Sometimes you'll learn quickly, or a song will come together easily and naturally, but a lot of times it will end up being frustrating. Almost none of the professional musicians I know enjoy practicing because it's fun all on its own; they enjoy practicing because it allows them to hone their craft and get to a point where playing music *can* be fun, because the work has already been done. They put in the work because they understand that without the work, the joy of performing a piece in a way that makes them and their audience happy won't happen. Because a lot of amateur musicians start out playing as a hobby, they expect that when they try to make the shift to being a professional (even in a limited capacity), it will still be as enjoyable as their hobby was, and frequently that's not the case. Learning a song on your own time for fun is a very different proposition than learning ten songs in a week because you've been hired to play a wedding that weekend, and you need to have a specific set list ready to go. Also, should music be your hobby, then picking up your instrument is always an option. Once you decide to invest the time and effort necessary to make it on a professional level, it's not an option, it's a responsibility, and that can make a lot of difference in the way you feel about it.

Even if a band doesn't fail on a professional level, personal differences can drive even the most successful and talented musicians apart as clearly demonstrated by the Beatles. Great friends don't always make the best coworkers, and sometimes pre-existing relationships can make some of the work of being in a band more difficult. How do you tell your best friend since middle school, without it devolving into a larger argument, that he's not carrying his weight and needs to put in more work? I've asked some individuals about their experiences in bands that have split up, and I hope they can serve as a good reference for what can happen when band members decide to call it quits, and hopefully help show you that just because the band isn't working as a band, it's not the end of the road for your career in music. Not if you don't want it to be, anyway.

Chris Arbisi of White Trash talked to me about what he did after the band broke up and what his mind-set was like. "I realized during the whole process of recording the record that I was a good musician, not a great musician, and I was twenty-one years old. I'd been thrown out into the world and I realized that I wasn't going to make a lot of money as a musician if I wasn't signed to a record deal.[29] So I started to get really involved in the recording end of things." He said that his time with the band had helped him recognize his passion for music and helped drive him towards his eventual career in recording. Chris related that, "As you get involved,

---

29 This is in 1991/1992.

you start to learn what part of the business really appeals to you." He ended up going to work in a recording studio that worked on television and radio commercials, and that part of what he ended up loving about it was how many musicians he got to work with on a regular basis. "One of the most rewarding parts of this business is that I got to work with some of the best musicians in the business. I've worked with jazz greats like Randy Brecker or Will Lee. They're all everyday people, and this is how they make their fast cash, by working on jingles." Being involved with White Trash helped Chris realize that his passions lay firmly with music, and he was able to turn those passions into a rewarding career in recording. Not everyone in his band followed the same path of finding other areas of the music world to work in, as he said that some of the guys from the band had gone into finance and at least one at worked at Q Prime Management for a time before starting his own restaurant. For those who want to believe that music will always triumph there is a sort of happy ending; in 2007 White Trash reunited, and they now play shows occasionally.

Currently Matthew Taylor is pursuing a graduate degree in music composition at the University of Miami, where I met him after his time with Moses Mayfield. I asked him what led to Moses Mayfield's breakup, and he told me, "I believe the biggest issue that hurt us was not everyone was on board with being on the road all the time. This came to a head when our lead guitarist got engaged and announced he'd be leaving the band six months later." Touring does make for a difficult lifestyle, and it can be hard to swallow that most successful touring bands will stay on the road anywhere from six months to well over a year. It's stressful at the best of times, and if everyone's not completely on board, it can cause small problems to escalate very quickly. Additionally, in the case of Moses Mayfield, "we just didn't handle the division of labor very well, and we didn't speak openly with each other, leading to resentment." Again, if responsibilities and expectations are discussed as the group is coming together, these types of problems can sometimes be avoided. Not always, and it's good to have a way for people who are feeling overwhelmed or unhappy to voice those concerns and perhaps even take some time off if they need to without sacrificing the group as a whole. As Matthew told me, "communication has to be clear and to the point when dealing with a group of people. Otherwise, things will fester."

The important thing to remember when a music-related project fails is that it is not necessarily a reflection on the quality of the project. Unfortunately, this is an industry where talent won't win every time. A failed attempt is no reason to assume you won't become successful in the music industry in some capacity, and it can be a learning experience. You get the chance to figure out what group dynamics will and won't work, how much work you're willing to put into your music career, what aspects of the business side of being in a band you're best at, and maybe take a shot at writing music. It can also help temper your expectations if you do decide to form another band and take another shot at the music industry. Maybe you do learn that you don't want to be a professional musician, and there's nothing wrong with that either. Just like everyone's not cut out to be a kindergarten teacher even if they like kids, not everyone who enjoys music or plays as a hobby has a future as a professional musician.

I don't write these things to be discouraging, and I encourage everyone to chase their musical dreams for as long as they want to. But it's not a secret that far more bands fail than succeed, and even bands that do succeed sometimes end up breaking up later. Maintaining a positive outlook—even if a band falls apart or a specific project fails—is important. There's always something to be learned from the experience, even if it's as simple as, "Don't ever work with *that guy* again." And while no one ever wants to plan for a breakup, if you're writing songs as a group, it's best to write down everyone's contributions so they're easy to sort out later. While no one intends to ever take their friends to court, time and feuding can do funny things to memory, and, under the right (or wrong) circumstances, what was once "I only helped out with a couple of lines, it's not my song" can turn into

"I should get half the writing credit on that." As in any business arrangement, if you're taking in money and signing contracts, you should have all your internal arrangements worked out in case the need to dissolve the group arises. Even if it's not drafted by an attorney, a basic document outlining responsibilities, writing credits, and how profits are divided will be extremely useful for helping to diffuse arguments. Make sure the signing is witnessed by a non-band-member who also signs and that each member has a copy of the agreement with at least one other kept on file in a secure location. It sounds heartless, but it's far nicer to have something in place than to risk a breakup that gets so ugly that none of the band partners ever want to work together again. Sometimes that outcome can't be helped, but the cleaner the break can be, the easier it will be on everyone.

Interestingly enough, the website LegalZoom offers a band partnership agreement on their website for a fee. This legal agreement was developed in part by Joe Escalante, a bass player for the Vandals and owner of Kung Fu records. He offers free advice on the LegalZoom Facebook page for people who submit questions in a feature called "Free Joe" and hosts a radio program, where he'll also give out legal advice and take questions, called *Barely Legal Radio*. If you're starting out and can't afford an entertainment attorney, these are a few good resources to check out if you've got questions that you can't find answers to anywhere else. This isn't an endorsement of those products or services, but if you're looking for something that might have a little more legal heft to it than what you can draft on your own, that's a good place to start.

Personal relationships and business relationships fail regularly, and a band is both. Because the industry is so uncertain and open-ended, relationships can become strained very quickly. Keeping a sense of perspective and maintaining good business practices is vital to help keep things as professional as possible and not let personal differences grow into professional failure. Even with keeping this in mind, some bands just can't be saved, but that doesn't mean your whole music career is doomed. Keep your eyes open, constantly assess what you're looking for out of your career and what other options might satisfy those goals, and make sure you get everything down on paper. The music world has room for a lot of people, and not all of them are musicians.

CHAPTER 14:

HOW TO BE A BETTER FAN

If you're reading this book and you're not a musician, chances are you're already a pretty good fan; you're curious about the industry and about independent artists specifically, and I'm betting that the preceding chapters have given you a pretty good idea of how to help support your favorite independent bands. It's more than just buying CDs and attending concerts, and bands should be aware of this as well and continue to reward fans who invest the time and money to help keep bands going even after they "make it." The best way to be a better fan is to find out what the band needs you to do, since not all my advice is applicable to every situation. Sometimes bands will ask fans for help directly, particularly if the fans live in a specific area the band is trying to target somehow, but other times it can't hurt to send along an e-mail saying that you're a big fan and would like to know how you can help support their work. Some bands may not have time to reply to inquiries like that, but they might just like knowing that they've got support out there if they need it. You never know, though; I've gotten an internship through nothing more than e-mailing a band and saying that I was a music-business student and would love to help them out if they needed it.

The first tip on how to support independent artists should also be the most obvious: pay for their music. I've heard a lot of arguments on this and expect to hear a lot more, but it is the most concrete way to show your support. Some independent artists offer free downloads for signing up for their mailing list or just as a way to get their name out there and find new fans. You should still find something of theirs to pay for, whether it's concert tickets, merchandise, or whatever. The more money an artist can make purely from being an artist, the more time they'll have to devote to their work and the more music they'll be able to make for fans like you. Also, having an income stream from their music is something artists can show labels or other corporate sponsors to demonstrate that they're a worthwhile investment.

Another thing you can do is advocate for the band. People are more likely to check out a new band on the recommendation of someone they know and trust than because they're moved to by a commercial or other forms of advertising. Post links to a band's website or videos on your wall, have their music playing on your iPod when friends come over, things like that. It's probably best to be subtle about it, since music is a fairly personal thing for most people, and being told that "you *have* to listen to this group because they're the best thing ever and you'll *love* them, I just know you will!" can have the opposite effect on a certain kind of person.[30] Sharing posts, re-tweeting, reblogging on Tumblr, or pinning on Pinterest are all easy ways to spread the word about your favorite band if you've got followers on those sites. The more links that you have to the band's website, the higher they'll rise in Google search results for terms that could link back to them.

Another way to be proactive about helping bands you like is to get involved with your local music scene. Even if the independent group you're

---

30 Full disclosure: I am one of those kinds of people.

a fan of isn't local, by going to local shows and becoming familiar with venues in your area, you can help the band if they're looking to do a tour. When I was working with jazz singer Nicole Henry, every time a fan from a different city e-mailed us to ask when Nicole would be playing there, we'd ask them what good jazz venues there were in their area. Information like this is valuable for artists when they're getting ready to go on tour, and they usually don't have the time or money to fully research all the available venues in every potential tour stop themselves, so recommendations from fans are great. It's even better if those fans have a relationship with the venue and, if the band is interested in playing in that area, can actually say to a manager, "Hey, I really like this band, and I think they'd be a good fit for this space, you should check them out."

While I was talking to Tim Nordwind for chapter 4, I asked him what OK Go's fans had done in the past that had really inspired the band or flattered them, and he referred to the fan-made versions of the "A Million Ways" video as being something that caught their eye and helped spread the song around to family and friends. It was inspiring for them; as Tim said, "I think we received three or four hundred videos of our fans re-creating that one video. It also sort of inspired us to make another one, which ended up being the treadmill video. At that point viral videos weren't really a thing, and we just saw that 'Wow, people enjoyed this that much, we should go make another one,' and that one got passed around even more." Beyond helping the band launch their video career, OK Go's fans have given the band a boost in unexpected ways, as demonstrated by the saga of Orange Bill, the goose. Tim told me "We made a video for a song called 'End Love,' and we did a twenty-four-hour stop-motion shoot in a park, and there are all sorts of uncontrollable elements, one of which was this goose that wouldn't stop following us around, so the goose was in most of the video. And people really responded to that goose, and it was a completely unplanned thing; we did not plan to have a goose in our video, we just couldn't get that goose to leave. Our fans really loved it, and they made a Facebook page for the goose, and all of a sudden the goose became like a celebrity in the OK Go world, and I thought that was a funny and clever thing for our fans to do, and it brought attention to our video in a way we never imagined. That's just sort of a small example of the way our fans have come up with ways to spread the word in general." The band is grateful for how involved their fans have been in their career, as Tim explained. "We're very lucky to have this interesting and fruitful online communication with our fans where we make something and in response they make something back."

Matthew Taylor of Moses Mayfield echoed some of Tim's sentiments, saying, "The fans were great; I'm still in contact with some of our more ardent ones. They always offered to put us up for the night or bring food." Gestures like these may not seem like much to the fans, but as demonstrated here, the band will usually appreciate the sentiment, even if they're not in a position to accept. And, obviously, offers like a free place to stay or dinner will be more important to young bands that don't necessarily have tour support behind them. Offering to put up Beyonce for the night so she doesn't have to pay for a hotel is still a nice thought, but it's not likely to be received in quite the same spirit.

The access that fans have to artists right now is something that has never been seen before, and the rules are, to a certain extent, still being developed. There's an expectation that what had previously been a one-sided relationship (loving an artist and never expecting to hear from them) will turn into more of a mutually beneficial relationship that might not be a friendship, exactly, but would feature more communication. And some bands have great social-media skills (or social-media teams) and are able to tweet back or send little Facebook messages to many of their fans. But if you're sending things out to a group you enjoy or an artist you just discovered, don't expect to get anything back or get disappointed if your tweets and posts go seemingly unnoticed. Even independent artists can receive hundreds of messages and notifications on Facebook a day, to say nothing of other social-media outlets, and numbers like that are simply overwhelming. This shouldn't discourage you from interacting with the accounts of artists or groups you enjoy; you absolutely should, but if you don't get a personalized response back, it's not a slight on you. Being an independent artist is incredibly difficult, and there are just not enough hours in the day for everything the artist may want to do.

The best kind of fan any band or artist can hope for is one who is engaged, enthusiastic, and sincere in their appreciation. If you've got that going for you, you're already doing a great job. Stay aware of what your favorite bands are up to, offer help if you're in a position to do so, and be a good advocate for them. Any reasonable band will love you just for that.

CONCLUSION

The biggest question being asked in the music industry at the moment is also the most obvious one: "What happens next?" It's being asked by artists, labels, and, perhaps most especially, fans. The truth is that there is no one path forward that's going to work out for every band or every label.

First and foremost, I think it's important for fans, artists, and industry insiders to understand just how much is asked of artists when they're pushed toward this "independent" route. It's best to approach the situation as though it were a small business, since the artists are basically going into business for themselves. Many small businesses fail, and those are often run by people who have more business knowledge and experience than your average musicians. More importantly, the music industry is an incredibly fickle one, and it's also one of the industries that will often betray those who are hard-working, talented, and business savvy. It's hard to predict what will or won't be in style by the time you get your record together (which is one of the reasons why the single route might be best for emerging artists) or even if the support your fans promised you will materialize when needed. The best thing for artists to do is to adjust their expectations. Making your

165

way independently means that you won't be filling stadiums, and you may not even be able to quit your day job.

Even bands that have are signed to major labels are expected to be involved in the business to a greater degree than in previous decades. One of the things that Matthew Taylor of Moses Mayfield told me when I asked if there was anything he was unprepared for when they signed with Columbia was, "We were unaware of the amount of self-promotion we had to do. We weren't prima donnas, but we definitely had an entitled view of our place at the label." He elaborated: "The only way to secure success in the music industry is to be an artist that works tirelessly, without looking for the label or other outside aid. Because [the music] business is run as a business, by businessmen and -women, your talent is not recognized as much as your effort (especially effort that yields a profit). You want to be a self-sustaining entity as quickly as possible." He concluded that while Moses Mayfield had been signed at Columbia, "We relied too much on the label, and our parents and friends." The level of promotion a label will offer varies widely from case to case, and artists who are used to self-promoting and mobilizing their fans to help spread the word can continue to count on that support even if the label's PR efforts fall short.

One of the best reasons for artists to be informed and knowledgeable about the music business hasn't changed with the advent of the digital era: the more you know, the harder it is for someone to take advantage of you. Because the bright lights of the entertainment industry draw a lot of hopefuls, there are many people who will prey on the under-informed to make a quick buck before stealing off into the night. If you're aware of copyright law, you can make sure you don't sign your rights away unknowingly. Well-informed artists make less appealing targets than those who sound like they're just desperate for someone to come and take over all the hard, businesslike stuff so they don't have to think about it. Even if that is your goal, staying guarded until you get to know someone (and never giving anyone money up front) will pay off in the end.

It's also worth remembering that while there are artists who have become successful managing their own careers, there are far more who have failed to have a profitable career. How you define success for yourself is different for every person, but it's best to keep your goals modest and focus on where you're successful rather than where you're not. It is still important to set goals and to not flail aimlessly. If you're going to start a Facebook page, how many fans would you like to have? What are you going to provide for your fans there that will keep them coming back and referring friends? Are you able to dedicate time every day to post and interact with people who have sought your page out? These efforts are a marathon, not a sprint, and managing your time wisely and taking on only what you know you can manage will be better than getting in too deep and ending up flaking on all your various projects because you feel overwhelmed.

There's been a lot of talk about making all music free via the Internet, and the way I personally feel about that changes depending on who is promoting that viewpoint. When musicians say they intend to give away their music because they'd rather people have it for free or on a pay-what-you-want basis than make a set amount of money per download, I think it's a great thing and a demonstration of the openness the Internet allows between creator and consumer when it comes to something like music. When people who aren't musicians or involved in the music industry talk about how music should be available on demand for free to anyone at any time, I wonder how one explains being a lover of music and at the same time considering it literally worthless. There's been a lot of excuses bandied about for people espousing this viewpoint, but it all boils down to "if I want to get the music for free, I can, so they should just make it free anyway," which fails to take into account the work that goes into creating that album or song and the fact that the people who created those works should be compensated. There are services out there that are helping us move more toward having the feeling of free music available anytime, anywhere while still operating in such a way that artists are compensated: services like

Rhapsody, Spotify, Muve, and others where you're not paying for individual tracks but for access to huge repertoires of music, which are then available to you in a variety of ways. As Internet access spreads and smart-phones end up in the hands of more Americans, these business models become more appealing to the music industry and to fans. The assumption has been that streaming services cut down on paid downloads, and, while that may be true to a small degree, many in the industry seem to be ignoring that for people who are interested in free streaming services the alternative isn't usually purchasing the song outright, it's pirating it from a torrent site or other illegal distributor. Spotify may pay you only fractions of a cent per stream, but even that's better than receiving no money at all. The push back from the music industry with the development of streaming services is not very different from the push back seen from the music industry when radio first entered the American marketplace, or the industry's resistance to adapting to digital downloads. Change is always uncomfortable and happens only because consumers demand it.

Making a career in music is hard. I don't mean to make light of that, and this book in no way guarantees success of any kind. Too many people seem to assume that people interested in becoming professional musicians are doing so because they're too lazy to get a "real" job. I won't deny that there are a lot of people who seem to think that being able to play guitar semi-competently means they don't have to acquire any real skills, or people who will wait around to be discovered rather than work hard on developing their career independently, and those people do give other musicians something of a bad reputation. The truth is that becoming successful in the music world takes a very strange combination of talent, perseverance, and luck that can't be bought, sold, or promised to you by anyone. The only common factor in the successful artists I've known is the huge amount of work they put in, day after day, even after they've reached certain career goals. Superstar artists aren't exempt from this, and anyone who thinks that people like Rihanna, Kanye West, or Justin Bieber live a life of leisure and ease haven't seen the kind of tour schedules that those stars (and their vast support staff) maintain. Sure, they could stop any time they liked and still be richer than most of us can ever dream of, but the people who do this usually can't stop. They want to play more shows, to get more fans, to find new opportunities to elevate their career. And the frustrating truth is that you can put in that work and you can have that drive and that passion, and it still won't work out for you. There are very few careers where one can genuinely say that no matter how hard you work and how much talent you have, you still may never succeed, and most of those careers are in the arts. Having a business plan in place increases the likelihood that you'll find some success or at least reap a little bit of money from your efforts, but nothing is certain.

There are some facts that can't be denied, though: for instance, people love music. Music is not going away, and therefore the music industry is not going away. Copyright is not going away, because the people who make music (as well as the other art forms covered by copyright law) by and large want to be compensated for their art as well as have the protections enshrined in copyright law. The next few years or decades are going to be very painful for a lot of artists and business people in the industry. Every week there's some hot new development, and the next week there are dozens of editorials on why that new development is not so hot or new and surely isn't worth the time to consider seriously. Paying too much attention to these reports will drive you crazy before long. If you want to make a living as an artist, the best thing you can do is keep doing what makes you happy the best you can.

APPENDIX A

Definitions Cheat Sheet

A&R—An abbreviation for "Artists and Repertoire."—traditionally, the department in a record label that handles finding, signing, and overseeing the artists under contract to the label.

Digital mechanical license—A mechanical license obtained for digital copies of a composition available for sale. Subject to the same rates and restrictions as a mechanical license.

Licensee—The artist or company that owns the rights to the work being licensed

Licensor—The individual or group seeking to license an artist's work

Master use license—The right to use the master recording of a song, usually sought in conjunction with a Synchronization License

Mechanical license—A license that gives permission to put a composition on a fixed medium available for sale. Requires royalties to be paid per copy sold, which at the current time is 9.1¢ per song or 1.75¢ per minute of playing time, whichever is greater.

Performing rights organization (PRO)—A group that collects performance royalties on behalf of the songwriters who register their songs with the group. The three performing rights organizations in the US are ASCAP, BMI, and SESAC.

Public domain—The terms for works that are no longer under copyright protection. There is a registry of cultural works that are in the public domain at PublicDomainWorks.net

Public performance—Any performance that is not conducted in a personal or non-public space. Includes playing the radio or playing music over speakers in restaurants, shops, and in some cases at public gatherings. Copyright law gives artists the right to specifically license Public Performances though these licenses are generally handled by **performing rights organizations** (see above).

SoundExchange—An organization that handles all digital performing royalties, which can be collected by songwriters and recordings artists. They are separate from the traditional PROs, so be sure that you're registered with them in addition to either ASCAP, BMI, or SESAC.

Square card reader—A device and app that can be used with smartphones to allow bands or other retailers to accept credit-card payments anywhere. Takes a small fee from all transactions, but requires no up-front cost.

Synchronization license—A license that gives permission for a composition to be used in an audiovisual medium, such as television or movies. The composition is literally synched with the video.

APPENDIX B

Resource Cheat Sheet

I mentioned a lot of different sites and other resources that can be helpful for young artists in this book, and in a lot of different places. For ease of use, I've compiled them alphabetically here, along with a brief description.

Bandcamp.com—A site that allows users to build custom pages with embedded songs, images, calendars, and other tools. Also provides analytics and a platform for selling merchandise in exchange for a percentage of sales.

CDBaby—An online service that specializes in creating CDs, download cards, and other physical products for bands to sell. They also offer digital distribution services. Pricing varies based on what products you're interested in.

CafePress—Merchandise service where you can design a logo or other graphic and choose what products you want to make it available on. Free, to set up a basic store account, and you have some leeway with pricing, with CafePress keeping a certain amount per item. Shopkeepers do get discounts on their own merchandise if you want to have some products to sell at shows.

CreativeCommons.org—A group dedicated to the free exchange of art and ideas and a way to easily license your work for use by others, using their six standard licenses that range from letting others use your work any way they want (even commercially, as long as they credit you) to only allowing others to download your work and share it as long as they credit you.

Digital Music News—Both a website and e-mail newsletter that stays on the cutting edge of music in the digital realm. Covers record labels, Internet radio, satellite radio, purchasing trends, and everything in between.

Indaba.com, MyOnlineBand.com, MusiciansCollaboration.com, and Kompoz.com—all sites that allow musicians and people seeking music to collaborate online on music projects.

Kickstarter—Crowd-sourced campaigns for creative projects ranging from the arts, to video games, to bands. Kickstarter must approve all projects, and if you don't reach your goal amount in the time you've set for the fundraising, then you don't get any of the money, but you're under no obligation to complete that project.

MosesAvalon.com/calculator—The royalty calculator mentioned in chapter 10.

SellYourBand.com—Site that features a large collection of a la carte resources for musicians. Download cards, merchandise, legal and fundraising tools, tools for creating mobile apps, and more can be found here.

TuneCore—A service that lets users upload their own music to sell as CDs or digital downloads; it acts as an aggregator for getting material onto iTunes and other digital distribution services. They operate on a fee per material uploaded, plus a percentage of sales.

Zazzle—Merchandise service similar to CafePress with the main difference being that Zazzle has a few more products available for customization.

REFERENCES

There are three books that have been invaluable to me in my music business education and I would recommend them to anyone interested in pursuing their own career in the industry, as an artist or otherwise. They are:

David J. Moser, *Moser on Music Copyright* (Boston: Thompson Course Technology and Artist Pro Publishing, 2006)

Greg Kot, *Ripped: How the Wired Generation Revolutionized Music* (New York: Scribner, 2009)

M,William Krasilovsky, Sydney Shemel, John M. Gross, & Jonathan Feinstein, *This Business of Music: The Definitive Guide to the Business and Legal Issues of the Music Industry* 10th Edition (New York: Watson-Guptill Publications, Nielsen Business Media, 2007)

Additionally, the daily newsletters from Digital Music News (free from digitalmusicnews.com) and Billboard's "Billboard Bulletin" are useful for keeping up with news and developments in the music industry overall. I found many of my sources or leads through the newsletters I received from one or both of those services. All other sources have been cited specifically in the text or in the footnotes.

ACKNOWLEDGEMENTS

First of all I'd like to acknowledge my family, especially Edward and Angelina Burgess (my mother and father) for their support and faith in me through my education and while writing this book. Everyone in my family has been nothing but positive and encouraging about this project, which helped more than I can say.

In addition to my family, my professors at the University of Miami were huge inspirations, particularly Rey Sanchez and Serona Elton. I would not be as interested in the music industry if it I hadn't had the pleasure of being in their classes. Rey Sanchez in particular is the person who gave me the inspiration to write this book and his guidance has shaped my aspirations in more ways than I have room for here.

I would like to thank everyone who agreed to be interviewed for this book; Timothy Nordwin, Matthew Taylor, Darren Paltrowitz, Chris Arbisi, and Michael Bouchard. All of them contributed information and insight on areas of the music industry I had little to no experience with and so I'm eternally grateful for their help.

I'd also like to thank the people who helped me find my feet in the music industry and be exposed to how independent artists do business;

Arielle Kilory and Nicole Henry were exceptional bosses and the experience of working in the world of independent artists is what lead to this book.

Finally, I'd like to thank everyone out there who bought this book, either for their own pleasure or for someone else. I wrote this for independent artists and in a lot of ways I'm an independent artist myself, and so I value each and every person who helps me along my way. The world would be a far less interesting place without artists or the people who appreciate them, so thank you for making the world more interesting, more beautiful, and more worthwhile.

On a more technical note: the music industry changes all the time, and all the resources and services I evaluated in this book were evaluated based on the information available to me at the time. Please be sure to investigate all available options based on your own needs and with the most up to date information you can find.

BIOGRAPHY

Genevieve Burgess earned her Bachelors degree in Music and her Master of Music Business and Entertainment Industries at the University of Miami's Frost School of Music. She has worked with OK Go and Nicole Henry as well as Cat 5, an independent student-run music publishing company. She has been a musician herself since she picked up a flute at eight years old. She regularly writes for several websites, including Pajiba, Not the It Girls, Persephone Magazine, and others. You can also find her on Facebook and Twitter.

www.ingramcontent.com/pod-product-compliance
Lightning Source LLC
Chambersburg PA
CBHW071153050326

40689CB00011B/2092